The Observologist

(actual size)

Giselle Clarkson

GECKO PRESS

The Observologist

Observology

- 4   OBSERVOLOGY: The Study of Looking
- 8   PRINCIPLES of OBSERVOLOGY
- 11   PREPARING for OBSERVOLOGY
- 12   KEEPING THINGS ORDERLY (Taxonomy)
- 14   SCIENTIFIC NAMES
- 16   OBSERVOLOGICAL INSTRUMENTS
- 18   AN OBSERVOLOGIST'S INTRODUCTION TO INVERTEBRATES (Anatomy)

Four perfect places to mount an observological expedition...

A Damp Corner

- 26   SLUGS and SNAILS
- 32   FUNGI
- 36   WOOD LICE
- 38   CENTIPEDES vs MILLIPEDES
- 40   PONDS and LONG-STANDING PUDDLES
- 42   THINGS TO SPOT AT NIGHT
- 44   PATIENCE
- 45   HOW TO GET A FLY TO GO OUTSIDE
- 46   HIDING IN PLAIN SIGHT

Pavement

- 50 ANTS
- 55 BIRDWATCHING WITHOUT BIRDS
- 56 COLLECTIONS
- 58 LICHEN
- 60 PHENOLOGY
- 62 DROPPINGS and EGGS
- 64 WORMS
- 68 HOW TO SAVE A WORM
- 69 HOW TO SNEAK UP ON A BUG

A Weedy Patch

- 73 BEES
- 75 HOW TO HELP AN EXHAUSTED BEE
- 77 COMMON WASP vs HONEY BEE
- 78 WASPS
- 80 THINGS TO FIDDLE WITH
- 83 WET DAYS
- 84 GROWING UP AS AN INSECT
- 86 CATERPILLARS
- 88 SEEDS
- 90 NOTABLE LEAVES

Behind the Curtains

- 94 COCKROACHES
- 99 FLIES
- 102 AURAL OBSERVOLOGY
- 104 SPIDERS
- 110 HOW TO RELOCATE A SPIDER
- 111 HOW TO SAVE A MOTH FROM DROWNING
- 112 MOTHS
- 115 MOTHS vs BUTTERFLIES

- 116 FINAL EXAM
- 118 INDEX

OBSERVOLOGY: The STUDY of LOOKING

Scientists who study nature often go on field trips and expeditions. They can spend days, weeks or months on windswept islands or mountainsides, at sea, in jungles or in polar regions.

An observologist is someone who makes scientific expeditions every day, albeit very small ones. They notice interesting details in the world around them. They are expert at finding tiny creatures, plants and fungi.

They know that earthworms have bristles...

I'm not bald!!! My hairs are just very fine.

and that moths come out in the daytime.

I'm not one of those late night party animals.

They know EXACTLY where to find a wood louse when they need one...

It's my time to shine!

PET WANTED
MUST HAVE 14 LEGS.
REWARD: $500.00

and how many tentacles a slug has.

No, no... this can't be right?

An observologist knows that there are fascinating things to be found in even the most ordinary places.

Many of these things are very, very small.

I'M RIGHT HERE!

And others are easily overlooked.

BORING SITUATIONS IMPROVED WITH OBSERVOLOGY

School

An adult bumps into someone they know

There's a power cut

It's lunchtime and your best friend is off school that day

"I'll just be a minute."

Indecision at the plant shop

=pluck=

Waiting for your turn

As if this isn't a perfectly sensible way to go for a walk.

It's very easy to become an observologist.

The FIRST, MOST IMPORTANT step

is to spend a lot of time gazing at the ground. A good thing about being young is that you're closer to the ground than most adults, so you have an excellent view of what's going on down there.

Another good thing about being young is that nobody thinks you're strange if you pay attention to a worm, an ant or a puddle. Adults tend to feel embarrassed doing that sort of thing. Hopefully you'll remember it's not worth worrying about what others think when you're doing what you enjoy.

The SECOND (also very important) step

is to be curious. An observologist is a detective, always on the lookout for a clue that will lead to something interesting.

Where is that caterpillar going? 
FOLLOW IT!

What's under that brick? 
LIFT IT UP!

Why is that leaf so holey? 
TURN IT OVER!

Why is the footpath white here? 
LOOK UP! (and close your mouth)

In this book you'll be introduced to four places that are perfect for mounting observological expeditions: a damp and mucky corner, concrete paths, an overgrown weedy patch, and inside your own home.

And if you ever find yourself apologizing for being late because you were busy waiting to find out what a caterpillar would do when it reached the end of the branch it was on, there's no doubt about it: you'll be a qualified observologist for the rest of your life.

It's a jungle out there

Leopard (slugs)

Tortoise (beetles)

Giraffe (weevils)

HUMANS ARE HUGE!

You might not even be the tallest person in your class, but to hundreds of thousands of animals you are a GIANT.

1. Think of the smallest animal you have ever met.

You could hold hundreds of ants in the palm of your hand (it'd be hard to keep them there though).

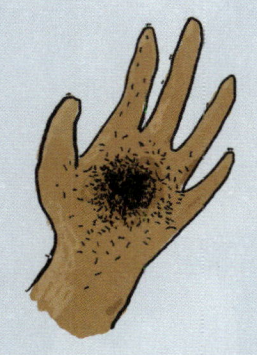

I beg you not to.

MIGHTY STEED! ONWARDS TO THE NEAREST LICHEN PATCH!

You could fit dozens of aphids up your nostrils.

You're so big compared to a tardigrade that you wouldn't even know if there was one in your ear.

2. Think of the BIGGEST animal you have ever met.

There isn't much room for me up your nose.

3. Then imagine what it would be like to meet a creature so big you could live your whole life on its back. To a tiny insect, that creature is YOU!

PRINCIPLES of OBSERVOLOGY

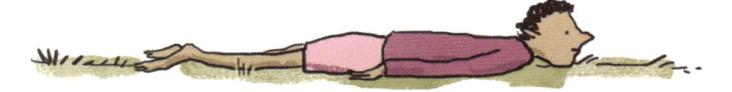

A POSSIBLE POSITION

Be curious! Peer into corners and underneath things. Look for overgrown edges and neglected nooks. Don't worry about looking silly. Get close to the ground and stay there.

Keep your body as still as possible so you don't scare things away.

Be patient! Try to resist the temptation to poke an insect in order to make it do something. It won't do anything cool while it's scared of you.

Never stick your fingers into places you can't see, like under a rock when you're about to turn it over. There might be a creature that bites or stings hiding under there.

And when you've finished looking under a rock, or a plant pot, or a piece of wood, always put it back the way you found it (taking care not to squash anything).

An unusual tree, but very nice.

(Just make sure you move before something spins a web or a cocoon on you.)

It's nice to let insects out of the house and save them from drowning in puddles, but be careful how much you interfere in their lives. A moth hatching from its cocoon might look as if it needs help getting out, but if it doesn't do it by itself, its wings won't unfold and it will never fly. It might be tempting to free a pretty beetle from a spider's web, but the spider might die if she doesn't eat that beetle.

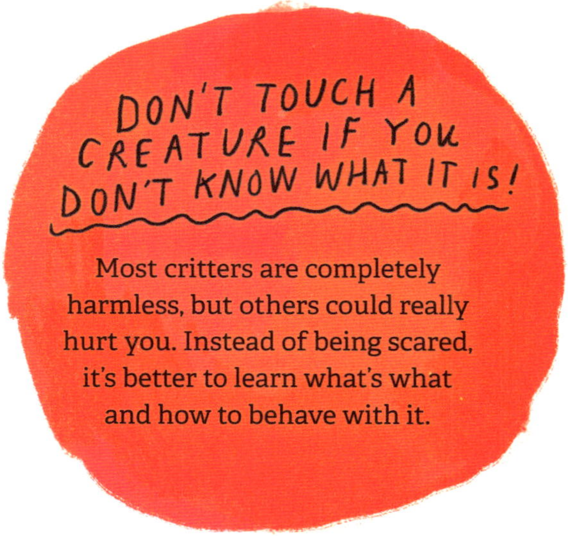

DON'T TOUCH A CREATURE IF YOU DON'T KNOW WHAT IT IS!

Most critters are completely harmless, but others could really hurt you. Instead of being scared, it's better to learn what's what and how to behave with it.

REASONS TO TURN OVER THIS LEAF

- Shiny dry slime
- Hole
- A curly-wurly poop
- Suspicious silhouette
- Yellow patch
- Chewed edges
- An ant
- Droppings

Snails and slugs have rasping mouths, particularly good for making holes in the middle of leaves

Stink bug

Stink bug eggs

A snail resting and digesting

Aphids sucking goodness out of the leaf and turning it yellow

Caterpillars have nibbling mouths and tend to make a more ragged edge than snails and slugs do

Ladybird eating aphids

Aha! A culprit!

Ant on its way to harvest the sweet liquid that aphids poop out

PREPARING FOR OBSERVOLOGY

If there aren't as many creatures cohabitating with you as you would like, you can improve your sorry situation.

1. Don't use fly spray or other household pesticides, if you can help it. Many insects and arachnids won't do any harm in our homes, but fly spray kills indiscriminately. Usually, you can just usher a fly out the window if you want it to leave.

Right this way, my good sir.

2. Put out a welcome mat. It doesn't have to be a mat, it could be a wodge of old newspaper or cardboard, or a plank of wood. Dampen a patch of grass, then lay the mat on it and wait. The grass underneath will die (so make sure no one's going to get cross about that), but if you're lucky, creatures like worms and wood lice will have moved in.

Lift the mat after a week or two to see what's underneath.

3. Leave food outside and see who comes to enjoy the free buffet. A shallow dish of sugar water (not deep enough for tiny things to drown in) might attract bees or ants. A smelly old cat-food tin might invite wasps or flies.

Now THIS is prime real estate.

KEEPING THINGS ORDERLY (Taxonomy)

You could think of all the life on our planet as belonging on one enormous family tree. That family tree has had billions of years to grow and evolve strange and wonderful new branches, resulting in all the magnificent species that surround us today—and it's still changing.

Don't mess with me, my cousin is a carnivore.

> A species is a group of living things that are similar enough to each other that they're able to breed.
>
> Taxonomy is the science of figuring out where each species belongs in that tree so we can understand the relationships between them. This is how we learn that an octopus is more closely related to a snail than we are.
>
> Each species is assigned a place in each of these seven categories: kingdom, phylum, class, order, family, genus and species. Taxonomists use a more complex version of this, which you might like to study one day, but this will do for now.
>
> Each kingdom can be divided into phyla, and each phylum can be divided into different classes, classes divided into orders, and so on.

You can use a mnemonic to remember the sequence. A mnemonic is an easy-to-remember sentence using the same first letters as the thing you want recall. You can come up with one yourself.

A good mnemonic for the seven categories could be:

Kangaroos Play Clarinets Outside Fenella's Garden Shed

An outrageous mnemonic would be:

Knowledgeable Physicists Cite Ontologically Fascinating Gnome Science

I simply will not move until I have deduced the meaning of life.

YOUR EVOLUTIONARY FAMILY TREE

You are not a plant, fungus or bacterium so you belong to the same **KINGDOM** as every other animal on the planet. It's called Animalia.

I am NOT a vegetable

Today's ambassador for the Kingdom is a sea cucumber.

Your **PHYLUM** is Chordata and you share it with hagfishes, newts and geese.

You're a mammal, so you belong to the **CLASS** called Mammalia.

Narwhal

Shrew

Those weird hairless cats

SOME of YOUR CLASSMATES

Are you beginning to see some similarities?

In your **ORDER** are all the Primates, like monkeys and lemurs.

Your **FAMILY** members are all Hominidae: gorillas, chimps, bonobos and orangutans.

Your **GENUS** is Homo and your **SPECIES** is sapiens.

I feel an enormous sense of belonging.

Pbbbt

SCIENTIFIC NAMES

The names that scientists use for plants and animals can look intimidating at first, but once you understand how they work they can be great fun to say AND you can use them to talk precisely about the flora and fauna you like.

Here are three animals, all commonly known as daddy-long-legs. They all have lovely long limbs, but they're completely different species! So if you're having a conversation with a friend about daddy-long-legs, how will you know if you're both talking about the same creature?

> **Cool words**
> FLORA = PLANTS
> FAUNA = ANIMALS

Daddy-long-legs 
AKA a cellar spider from the genus *Pholcus*

Daddy-long-legs 
AKA a harvestman from the *Opiliones* order

Daddy-long-legs 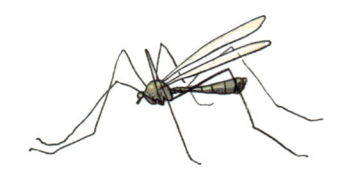
AKA a crane fly from the family *Tipulidae*

Counting legs and noticing where a creature lives is excellent observology, and a very important part of identifying a species. You can use this knowledge to find out their scientific name in a book or on the internet. Every species is given a unique one, so if you talk about *Pholcus phalangioides* (the spider, above left) there'll be no confusion about what you're describing.

"You know, the one with eight legs that lives on the ceiling."

"What? I thought you meant the one with eight legs that lives on the ground."

"Eh? I thought you were talking about the one with SIX legs flying all over the room."

Scientific names always have two or three words. The names are invented by scientists and often use Greek or Latin words that describe something about the species or the person who discovered it. You might be surprised by how many scientific names you already know, like this one:

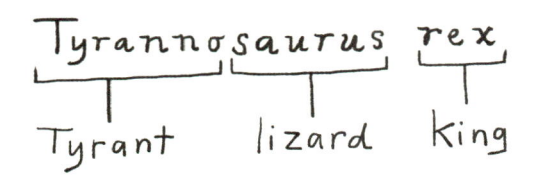

Tyrannosaurus rex
Tyrant — lizard — king

Here are some nice ones to say out loud:

Boops boops
(beau-ops beau-ops)
Cow eye

Wunderpus photogenicus
(wonder-puss photo-jen-ick-us)
A wonderous, photogenic octopus.

Upupa epops
(you-pooper ee-pops)
This scientific name comes from two old names for this bird, commonly known now as a hoopoe.

Turdus philomelos
(turd-us fill-o-mel-oss)
"Turdus" is an old Latin name for thrushes, and in Greek mythology Philomela is a woman who got turned into a songbird.
← Eurasian song thrush

Bittium **Ittibittium**
Two genera (the plural of "genus") of really tiny sea snails.

Two really small beetles. "Gelae" sounds like "jelly". Scientists are funny.
Gelaefish
Gelae baen

OBSERVOLOGICAL INSTRUMENTS

What's wonderful is that you don't actually need anything to be an observologist, besides your own senses. But a few things are handy to have.

A MAGNIFYING GLASS

You're accentuating my best feature... my entire body!

For seeing things you didn't know were there. You'll need something that keeps still long enough for you to get a really good look, though, like a dead fly, a resting caterpillar, a fungus or an egg case.

A SMALL MIRROR

I'm even better looking than I thought!

Keep one in your pocket for seeing around corners. You can hold it above your head to look inside a bird's nest, or low to the ground to see the underside of a fungus.

A CAMERA

Did you get my good side?

With a camera (like those on phones) you can "capture" the things you see. Digital photos keep a record of the time and date that you took them, which can be very helpful if you're indulging in a bit of phenology (see page 60).

A LITTLE LIGHT

A light can help you find interesting things in the dark. If it has a red light setting, even better. Red light doesn't bother nocturnal creatures the way bright white light does and is less likely to scare them away.

I appreciate being cast in such a flattering light.

DRAW WHAT YOU SEE

Sitting still long enough to draw a picture helps you to notice many tiny details. It also gives you something to do instead of just staring.

Are there shiny patches or hairy bristles? Can you see speckles or patterns? Is it brown like a chocolate biscuit or brown like a cardboard box? Don't worry about what your picture looks like; all that matters is the detail you notice while you're working on it.

Of course, it's easiest to draw things that keep still for a long time. Some good options are:

Parts of a dead insect that have fallen out of a spider's web

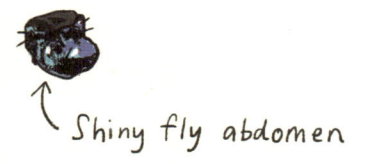

← Tiny wing

← Shiny fly abdomen

A branch with a lot of moss and lichen growing on it

← Is your branch truly brown or does it have some purple, red or blue?

A plant (like this dandelion) that you could revisit and draw every day to see it change from this to this.

When drawing spiders and insects, pay extra attention to how their legs bend. It can be confusing!

Incorrect, but funny

AN OBSERVOLOGIST'S INTRODUCTION TO INVERTEBRATES (Anatomy)

Most of the creatures you'll be observing are invertebrates: the name for all animals that do not have a backbone. Vertebrates are animals that do have a backbone—like birds, lizards, fish, and you. Most invertebrates are small. Bigger bodies would have trouble holding together without bones.

INVERTEBRATE ELEPHANT

The largest invertebrate on the planet is the colossal squid.

Are you calling me spineless???

There are also some pretty big crabs out there.

Unless you live under the sea, most of the invertebrates you meet will be insects, arachnids, mollusks and annelids.

Humans and horses are both mammals, made up of the same fundamental body parts, but I think you'll agree they take quite different forms.

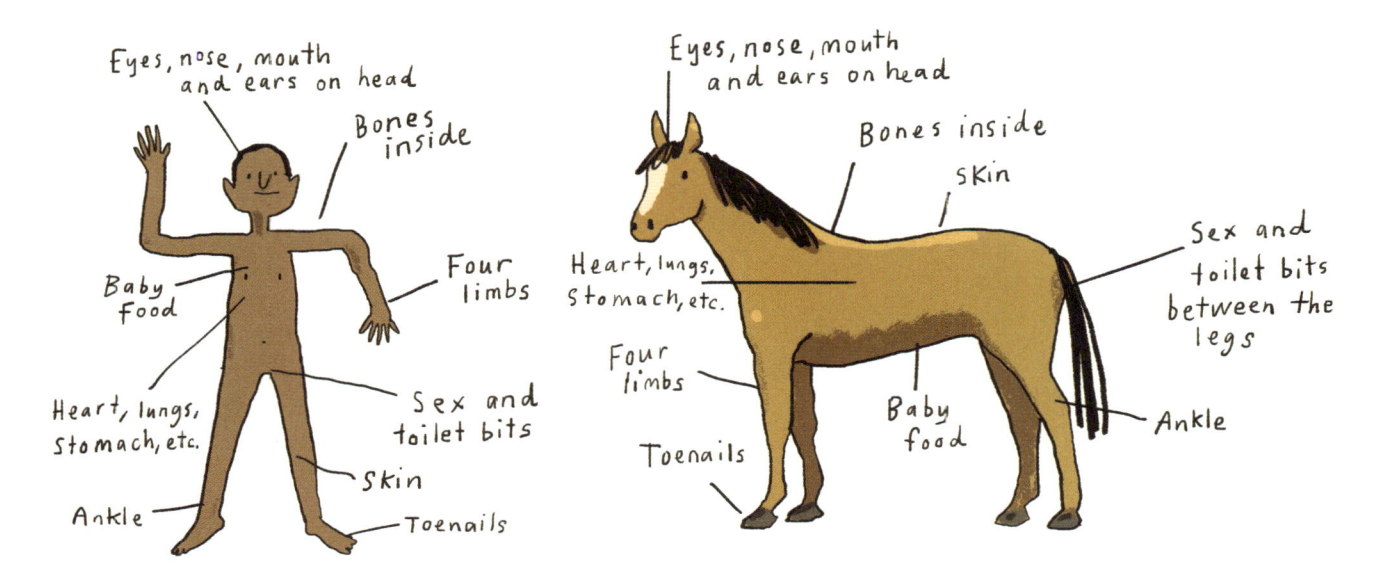

Insects are a bit like this too. This diagram shows typical insect body parts and the order in which they're put together.

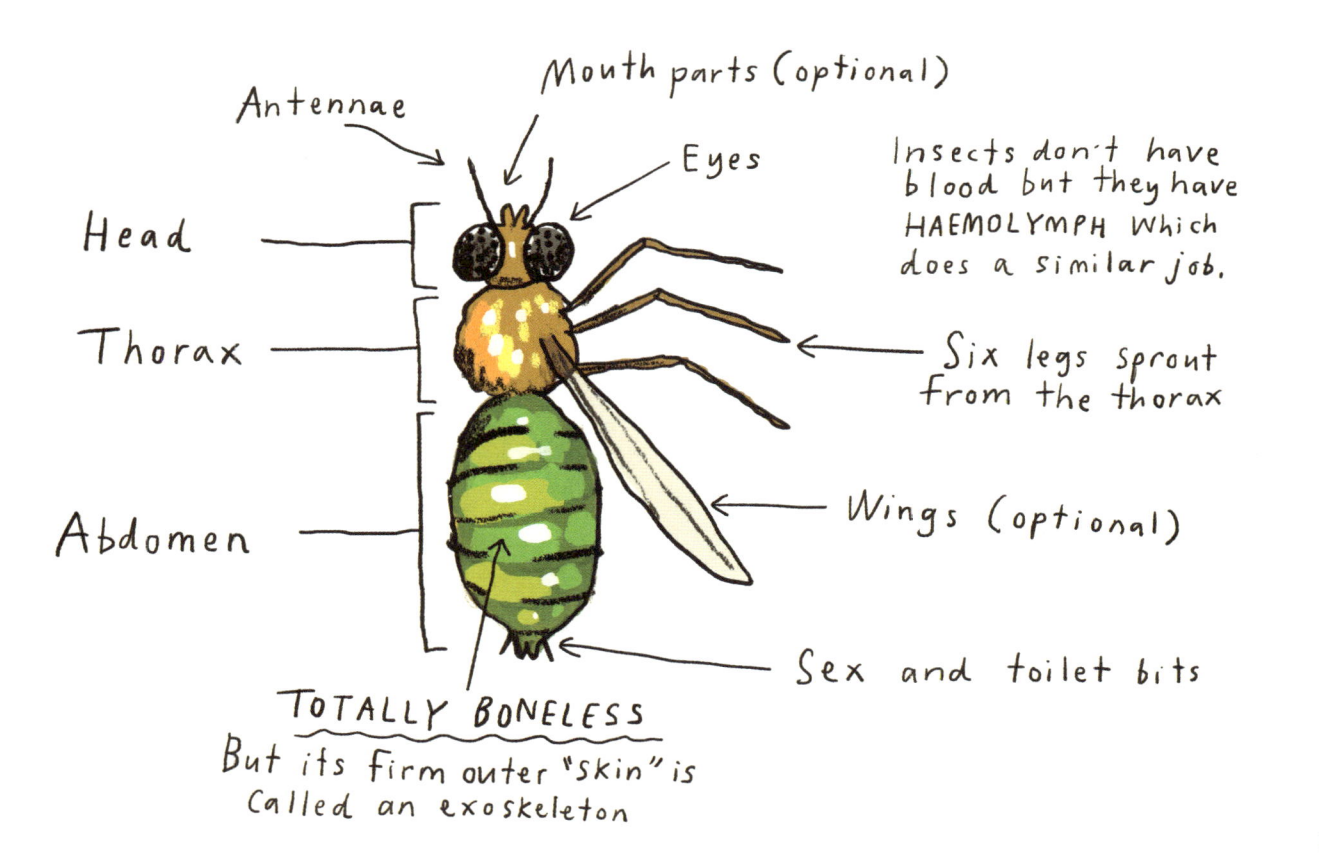

Not all insects follow this pattern, but when you're learning, it's very helpful to know your abdomens from your thoraxes. Here are some examples.

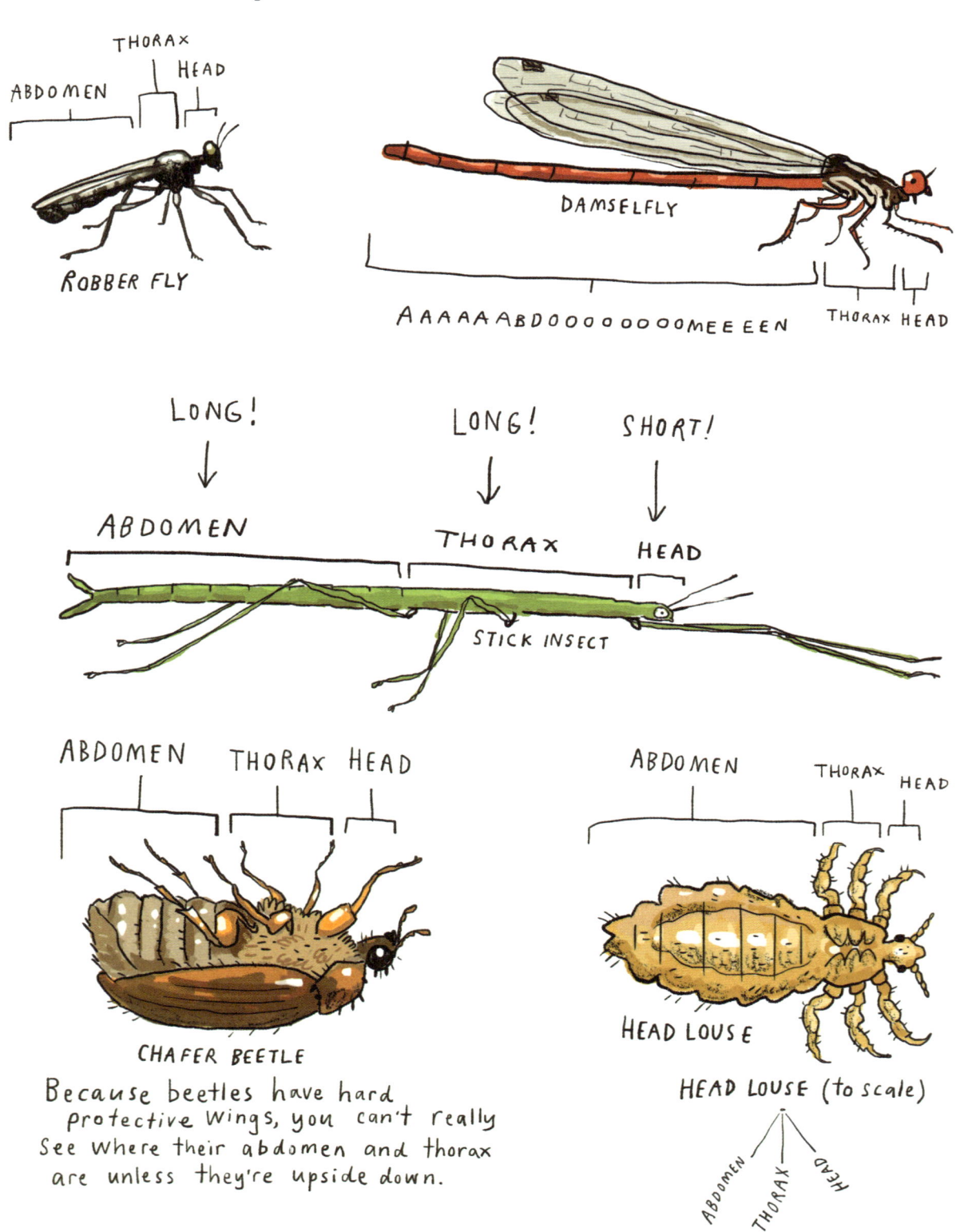

ABDOMEN | THORAX | HEAD

ROBBER FLY

DAMSELFLY

AAAAAABDOOOOOOOOOMEEEEN | THORAX | HEAD

LONG! ↓ ABDOMEN

LONG! ↓ THORAX

SHORT! ↓ HEAD

STICK INSECT

ABDOMEN | THORAX | HEAD

CHAFER BEETLE

Because beetles have hard protective wings, you can't really see where their abdomen and thorax are unless they're upside down.

ABDOMEN | THORAX | HEAD

HEAD LOUSE

HEAD LOUSE (to scale)

ABDOMEN THORAX HEAD

20

Spiders aren't insects, so their bodies are a little different. Insects belong to the phylum Arthropoda and the class Insecta. Spiders are arthropods too, but their class is Arachnida and we call them arachnids.

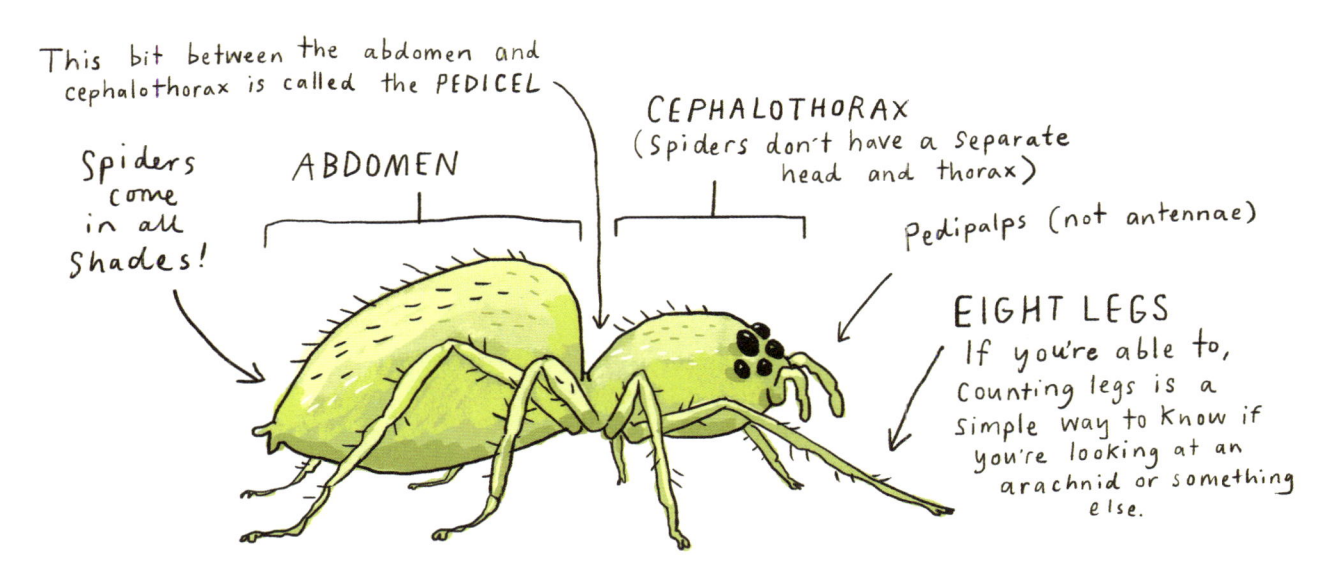

This bit between the abdomen and cephalothorax is called the PEDICEL

CEPHALOTHORAX (Spiders don't have a separate head and thorax)

ABDOMEN

Spiders come in all shades!

Pedipalps (not antennae)

EIGHT LEGS
If you're able to, counting legs is a simple way to know if you're looking at an arachnid or something else.

Centipedes and millipedes aren't insects either. And even though they look similar, with their long bodies and many legs, they belong to two different classes: Chilopoda and Diplopoda. You can learn to tell the difference between them on page 38.

Segmented body

Vast number of little leggies

Lovely legless slugs, snails and worms are not insects; in fact they're not even arthropods! Slugs and snails are mollusks (from the phylum Mollusca) and worms are annelids (from the phylum Annelida). There's more about their anatomy on pages 28 and 65.

Excuse me, are you looking for a roommate?

A particularly spectacular Philippine fried egg worm (Archipheretima middletoni)

WHAT IS IT LIKE TO BE AN INVERTEBRATE?

We don't know what it's like to be anything other than a human, so it's easy to think that the way we experience the world is the normal way. We see with our eyes, smell with our nose, listen with our ears, taste with our tongue, and feel with the nerves in our skin. But other creatures we meet have senses in VERY different places. After all, invertebrates don't even have a nose.

This cake is DELICIOUS

Butterflies have taste receptors on their feet.

Many insects have compound eyes that can see backwards and forwards at the same time. A compound eye is made up of ommatidia, microscopic hexagonal tubes that pick up light from whichever direction they're pointed towards. Dragonflies have up to 30,000 ommatidia, so sneaking up on one is incredibly difficult.

I've got no eyelids so I can't close my eyes at the scary part.

Spiders pick up sounds by feeling vibrations in the delicate hairs on their legs.

Your secrets are safe with me, though.

An insect doesn't breathe through its mouth; it has breathing holes on its body called spiracles.

Bees can see light at wavelengths that are invisible to us, so their world must look very different from ours.

Roses are luminurquoise, Violets are mauvescent...

Almost all insects have two antennae (or feelers) on their head. Different insects use them for different things, but their purposes include smell, taste, touch and communication. They come in many fetching styles.

FANCY FANS
(Lamellate)

BENT
(Geniculate)

FEATHERY FRONDS
(Plumose)

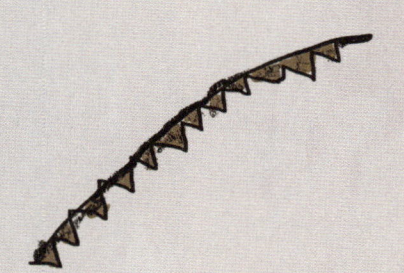

TOOTHY
(Serrate)

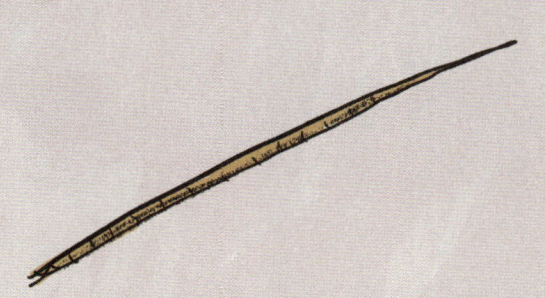

MINIMALIST
(Setaceous)

WIDER-AT-THE-TIP
(Clavate)

BUBBLY
(Moniliform)

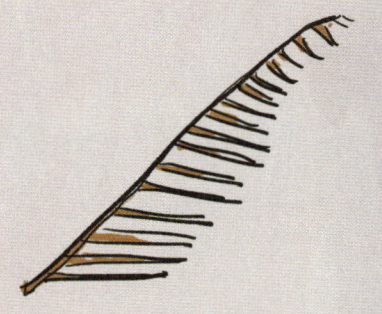

COMB-LIKE
(Pectinate)

To an observologist, a damp corner is full of promise. The shady side of a building where the sun barely touches, or the back of a garden where the hedge is thick and no one has weeded—if it's neglected, dim and never really dries out, it's wonderful. The best damp spots include nooks and crannies where creatures can hide. If you find long-lasting puddles or old containers that have filled up with water and fallen leaves, even better. These are the places you'll find nocturnal creatures hiding during the day, slimy things, fresh fungi, and insects that need water in order to breed.

A DAMP CORNER

SLUGS and SNAILS

Slugs and snails are so calm and silent, watching them can be very relaxing. They are mollusks, so their cousins include octopuses and the colossal squid. More specifically, they belong to the class Gastropoda, so we can call them gastropods if we like. Many gastropods live completely underwater, but terrestrial (land-based) gastropods only need their habitat to be a bit soggy.

MAGNIFICENTLY BRIGHT

Glaucus atlanticus BLUE SEA DRAGON
Spends most of its life floating upside down on the surface of the ocean.

Nembrotha kubaryana VARIABLE NEON SLUG
Lives on tropical reefs.

Sea slugs are amazing and some are really flamboyant. The only trouble is that they're difficult to visit, which is where land slugs excel. As the home observer might say, "A slug in the hand is worth ten in the sea." There is a lot to admire about a land slug when you take the time to look.

MAGNIFICENTLY ACCESSIBLE

Deroceras reticulatum GREY GARDEN SLUG
Beloved by those who marvel at a slug's graceful beauty, not beloved by gardeners.

"In my view, the meaning of life is very simple."

Limax maximus
LEOPARD SLUG

Lives in damp spots and is not a fussy eater. Enjoys munching on rotten leaves as well as other animals' turds.

A GASTROPOD

Meaning: STOMACH   FOOT

SNAIL PARTS

Most terrestrial gastropods are hermaphrodites; there's no such thing as a female or a male garden snail. Each snail has both male and female reproductive organs inside it, and can make both sperm AND eggs.

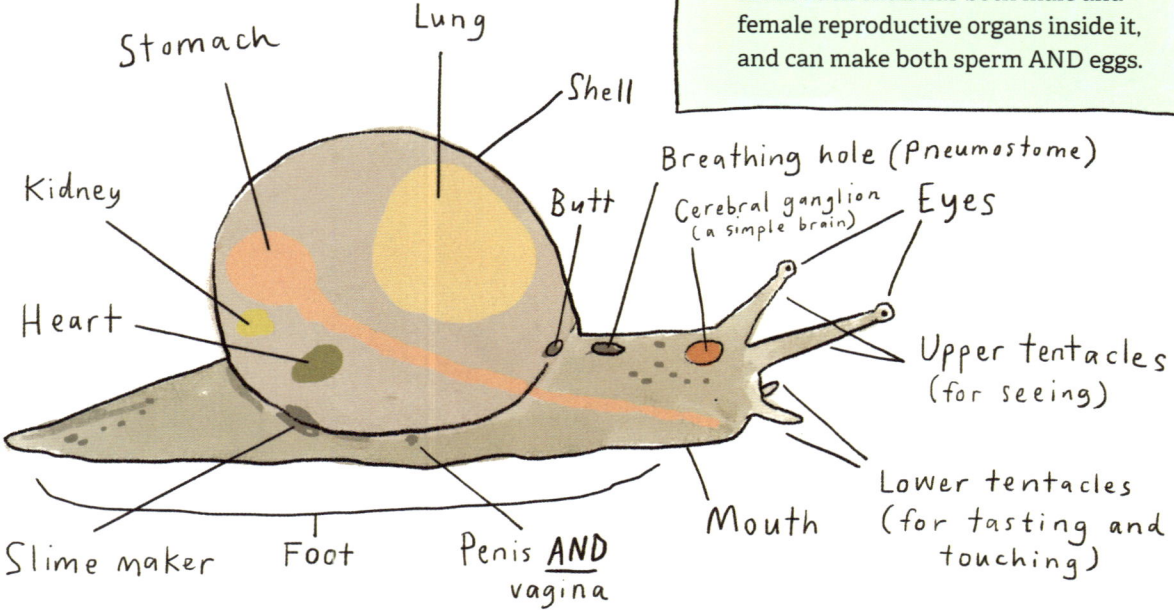

Labels: Stomach, Lung, Shell, Kidney, Breathing hole (Pneumostome), Butt, Cerebral ganglion (a simple brain), Eyes, Heart, Upper tentacles (for seeing), Lower tentacles (for tasting and touching), Mouth, Penis AND vagina, Foot, Slime maker

Slugs have many of the same body parts as snails, but with notable features of their own.

This thick bit that looks like a saddle is called the MANTLE.

It's usually pretty easy to spot a slug's pneumostome—it's only on one side.

Some slugs don't really have a visible mantle, like this Mt Kaputar pink slug from Australia.

"IS THIS DIGNIFIED?"

Put a slug on clear glass and watch the way its body ripples as it moves. It doesn't inch forward like a caterpillar or worm—it glides perfectly smoothly by contracting and releasing tiny muscles in a wave-like motion.

"Looking for something? I'll keep an eye out!"

Slugs and snails have fully retractable tentacles. Imagine having a body part that did that!

Slugs and snails do all their activities at night but you can see them during the day if you know where to look.

THE NEGLECTED MARGINS

UNDER THE RIM OF PLANT POTS

AT THE BASE OF SMOOTH, SLIPPERY PLANTS

A NICE, COOL LETTERBOX
(they will eat your mail indiscriminately)

CLUSTERED AROUND A SHADY, DAMP DRAIN

IN NOOKS AND CRANNIES

IN A CORNER

All these pretty shells belonged to different types of sea snails. Garden snails have beautiful, intricately patterned shells too—they're just so familiar that we don't always notice them.

Almost all garden snails have a shell that spirals on their right side. Very VERY rarely a snail hatches with a sinistral shell, meaning it spirals on their left.

Shells from sea snails

Did you get dressed in the dark?

RIGHT-SHELLED SNAIL   LEFT-SHELLED SNAIL

If you're studying a slug, take care not to let it get too dry or it will run out of slithering slime. It can't protect itself the way a snail can.

This is a crusty film called an EPIPHRAGM. The snail can create one of these to prevent moisture loss when it's very warm.

This is a *Theba pisana* snail, native to the Mediterranean.

Oi!

Don't yank a snail by its shell, you might hurt it! The kindest way to pick up a snail is to let it crawl onto something like a leaf, then pick up the leaf.

It can be fun to let a garden snail walk over your skin, just to see what it feels like. You'll get slimy, but that's fine—you can wash the slime off afterwards.

Cornu aspersum
THE COMMON GARDEN SNAIL

Magnificent

FUNGI

Fungi aren't plants. They're not animals either; they are entirely themselves. They have their own kingdom, and it's estimated there could be as many as 3.8 million different species—most of them haven't been studied by scientists yet.

Fungi are a vital part of a healthy ecosystem because they're absolutely wonderful at recycling. They typically do this by feeding themselves a diet of dying plants and then releasing nutrients that new plants can use. Many species even connect their mycelium (see opposite) with the roots of plants, taking sugars from the plant and giving water and nutrients in return.

Fungi love moist habitats, so you'll see them more often in warm, wet months than in dry, sunny ones. If you're looking for a fungus in town, pay attention to garden beds with tree mulch on them. There's a good chance that something interesting will pop up there.

We think of mushrooms as being edible and toadstools as being poisonous, but scientifically there is no such thing as a toadstool. If it's shaped like a mushroom, it's a mushroom. BUT not all mushrooms are edible and many are poisonous—eating even a tiny amount of a poisonous mushroom can kill you.

FOR YOUR EYES ONLY!

Unless a fungus has come from a food shop, you should appreciate its magnificence with your eyes and leave your fingers and mouth out of the equation.

FUNGI COME IN ALL KINDS OF STRANGE AND WONDERFUL SHAPES

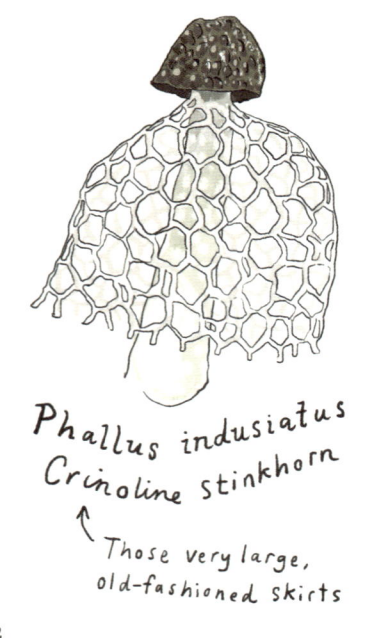

Phallus indusiatus
Crinoline stinkhorn
← Those very large, old-fashioned skirts

Clavaria zollingeri
Violet coral

Cyathus striatus
Bird's nest fungus

Armillaria novae-zelandiae
Glow-in-the-dark mushroom

PARTS OF Agaricus bisporus
THE MUSHROOMS IN THE SUPERMARKET

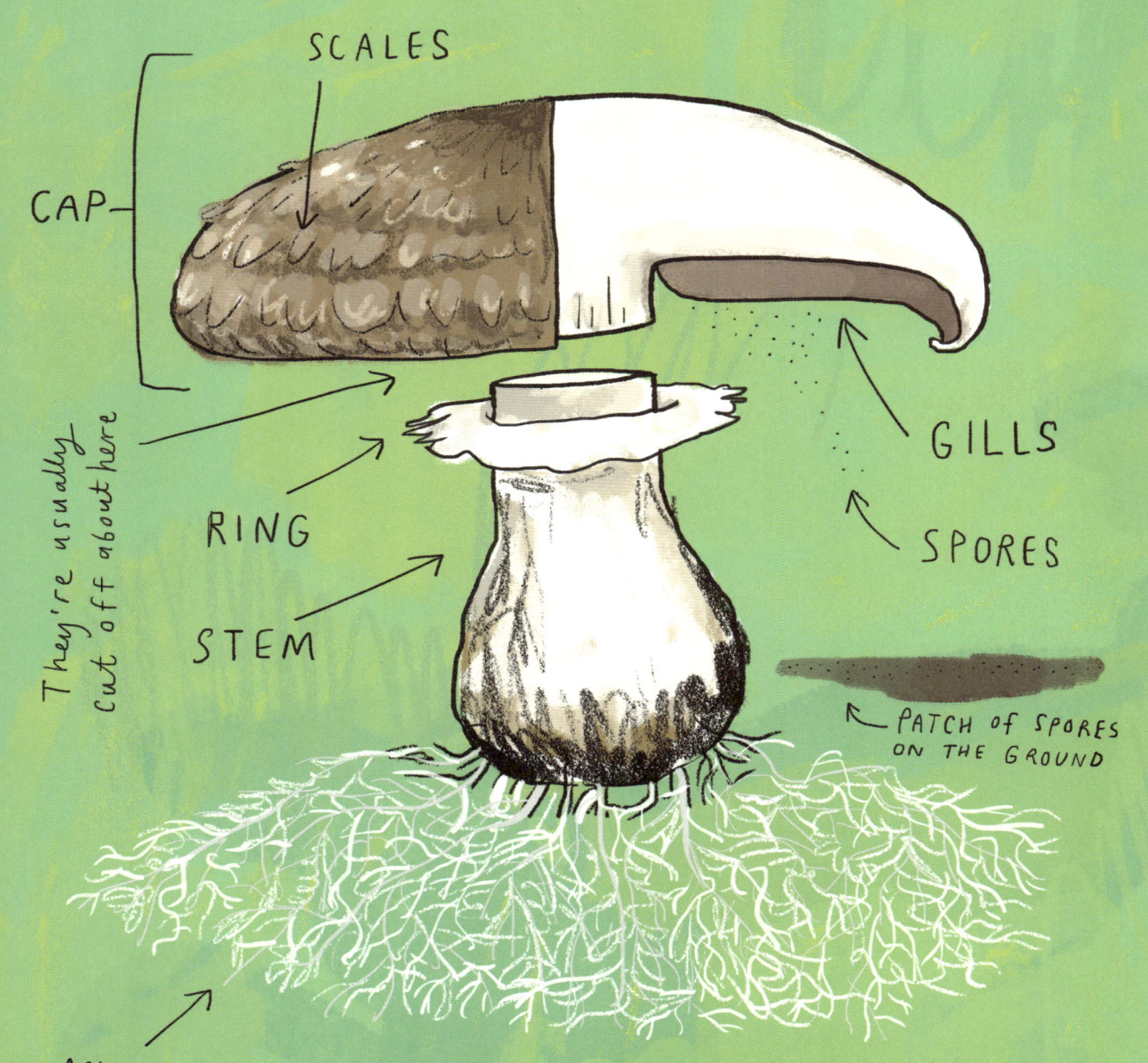

- **CAP**
- **SCALES**
- **RING** — They're usually cut off about here
- **STEM**
- **GILLS**
- **SPORES**
- **PATCH OF SPORES ON THE GROUND**

MYCELIUM (they're not roots!)
This is actually the main part of the fungus. The mushroom that we see is just the bit that grows in order to release spores for reproduction.

33

This spotty mushroom is probably the most famous fungus in the world. Just about everyone recognizes it, but not everyone knows its name. It's called *Amanita muscaria*, or fly agaric, because of its traditional use as an ingredient in fly traps.

A fungus on a fungus!

Instead of gills, some mushrooms have pores like a sponge.

Lots of small creatures like to eat fungi. Look very, very closely and you'll see tiny beetles, grubs, snails and slugs having a feast.

LITTLE BROWN MUSHROOMS (LBMs)

Identifying different species of fungi can be so tricky that sometimes even experts struggle to know which is which without studying them in a laboratory. There are so many types of little brown mushroom that that's exactly what scientists call them when they're not sure precisely what sort of little brown mushroom they are. So, if you find one, you can say with confidence: I have found a Little Brown Mushroom!

EVERYDAY FUNGAL ENCOUNTERS

Inside a compost bin

The silky white layer covering Camembert cheese

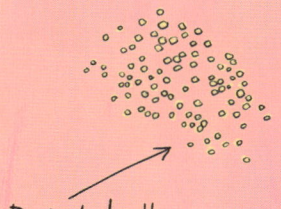

Dried balls of yeast from a packet

Yeast is a type of fungus. Thank a fungus for warm, crusty bread!

Microscopic wild yeast in the air all around us

A delicate, wispy fungus growing on a dog poop

When you forget to empty your school lunch box for a couple of days

WOOD LICE

A.K.A Slaters, sowpigs, johnny-grumps, bibblebugs, roly-polies, monkey peas, granny greys, chuggiepigs, butchy boys, granfer grigs, tiggy-hogs, rolinto balls, curly-buttons (and many more).

Wood lice (or slaters) are small, blue-grey terrestrial crustaceans. Crabs, crayfish and shrimp are crustaceans too, and wood lice are their cousins who live on land.

Although they left the sea behind, wood lice need to stay slightly moist at all times, so they live in damp spots: among shady leaf litter, in log piles or underneath plant pots. You're most likely to see them walking around at nighttime.

You'd never catch ME using a hairdryer.

Dear cousin Anita, I have been considering how different my life might have been were I endowed with magnificent pincers like yours. I suppose I should be happy that I am not delicious like you — did you know I taste of urine? Anyw...

They're a bit like tiny armadillos because they have tough, segmented "plating" protecting the body. When they get frightened, some species roll into a tight ball. They're easier to gently pick up when they're like this. If you stay very still with them in the palm of your hand, when they feel safe they'll walk around and tickle your fingers. They won't bite you.

Underneath a hedge would be a good place to look.

A wood louse next to a pea (actual size)

Porcellio scaber
pig — *little* — *rough (because of its knobbly texture)*

- Segmented dorsal plates
- A gentle nature and shy disposition
- Compound eyes
- Uropods
- Antennae
- Seven pairs of hairy legs for scuttling

Wherever you find slaters there's a good chance you'll find one of these spiders too. Slaters are almost the only thing they eat.

Dysdera crocata — Wood louse spider

"Imagine the feast I'd have, if only a giant lobster would crawl under my rock..."

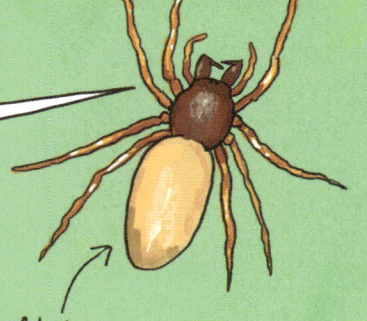

- Abdomen kinda looks like a peanut

37

CENTIPEDES vs MILLIPEDES

Centipedes and millipedes both have a lot of legs and you'll often find them living in the same place. So next time you're rummaging in the leaf litter, here's how to tell them apart. *Cent* means a hundred and *milli* means a thousand, but there are centipedes with about thirty legs, and only one kind of millipede has more than a thousand.

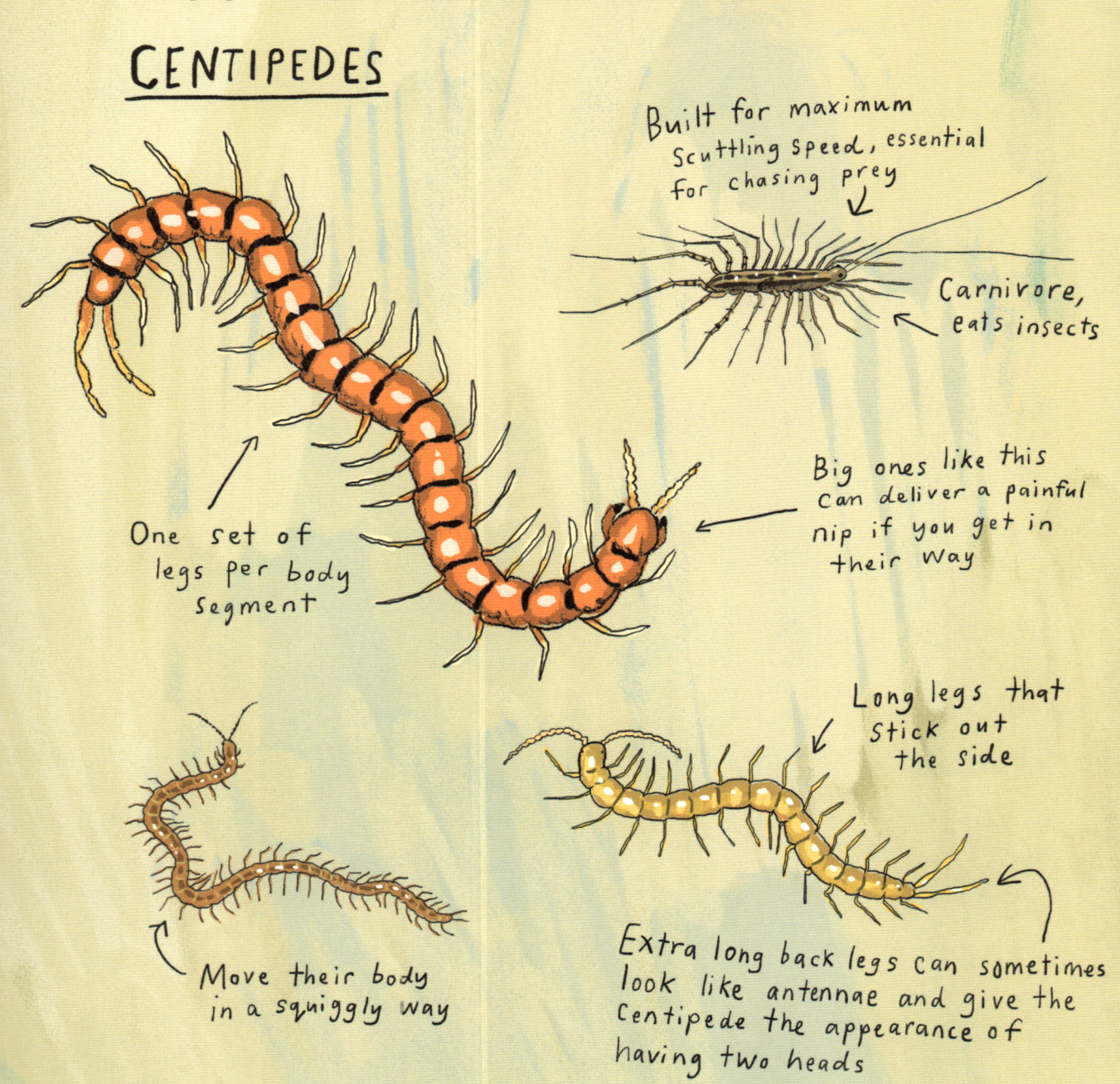

CENTIPEDES

Built for maximum scuttling speed, essential for chasing prey

Carnivore, eats insects

One set of legs per body segment

Big ones like this can deliver a painful nip if you get in their way

Move their body in a squiggly way

Long legs that stick out the side

Extra long back legs can sometimes look like antennae and give the centipede the appearance of having two heads

MILLIPEDES

← Vegetarian, eats decomposing plants

← TWO sets of legs per body segment

Built for tunneling ↓

Won't bite you ↓

← This one's an African giant millipede. It's over 30cm long!

↑ Their legs sprout from underneath their body (Centipede legs grow out their sides)

They curl up like this when they're scared →

Pill millipedes are only short and are easily mistaken for wood lice at first glance ↓

HUP! TWO THREE FOUR FIVE SIX SEVEN EIGHT NINE...

Much slower than a centipede and moves in a straighter line, like a train

PONDS and LONG-STANDING PUDDLES

Ah—the dampest spot of all! A pool of undisturbed rainwater is a magnificent habitat for all kinds of things.

FRESHWATER SNAIL

Little freshwater snails can walk upside down on the surface tension of the water. That's a very good party trick. When they want to, they can let go and float gently into the depths below.

Similar to a water boatman but it swims with its belly facing up

BACKSWIMMER

WATER BOATMAN

This little aquatic insect is called a water boatman because its legs look like oars paddling it through the water.

PLANKTON

People mostly think of plankton as living in the ocean, but there's also plankton in fresh water. They're so small you might not be able to see them at all with your naked eye. You need a microscope to get a really good look. The one in this close-up on the left is called a copepod and it has only one eye.

EXTREME CLOSE-UP

A leech looking for some blood to suck

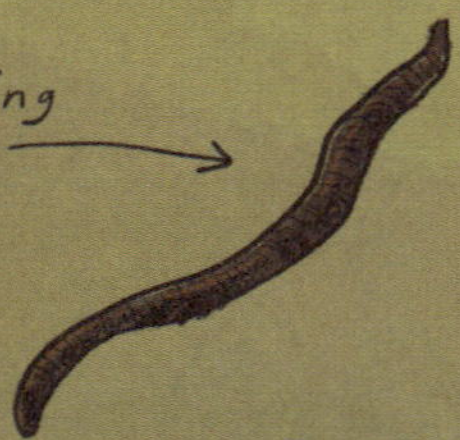

A raft of mosquito eggs

A good spot for catching mosquitoes and other insects attracted to water

← Adult mosquito

MOSQUITO LARVA

Moves in a very wriggly manner

MOSQUITO

Mosquitoes are a type of fly. They don't have maggots like a blowfly; instead, their larvae swim around in still, fresh water.

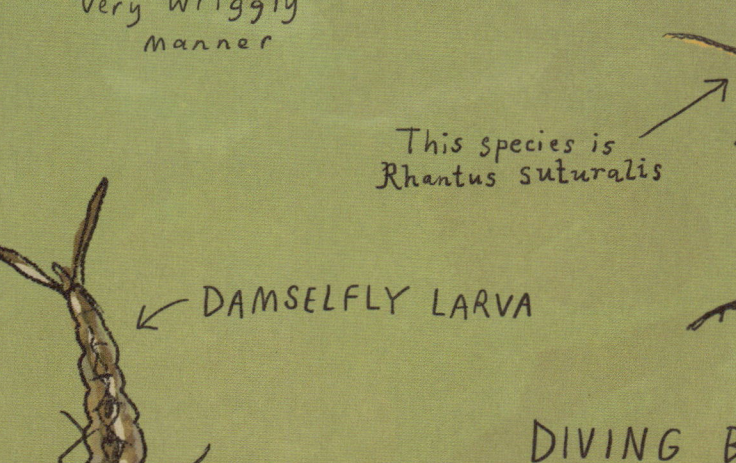

This species is Rhantus suturalis

← DAMSELFLY LARVA

Has an air bubble under its wings

DIVING BEETLE

There are beetles that live underwater! They carry a bubble of air for breathing, like tiny scuba divers. If they want to move to a new pool, they simply fly there. This one's going to eat that mosquito larva.

Aquatic worms waggling around in the sediment

THINGS to SPOT at NIGHT

Many animals do their essential business during moonlit hours. Then, you'll see all sorts of things eating, being eaten, mating and sometimes even being eaten while mating.

Doing some darning

Moths have eyes that glow when you point a light at them. You might see two tiny glowing beads peering at you out of the grass long before you see the rest of the moth's body.

Snails will be out and about, enjoying not being dried out by the sun. The same goes for slugs. You might even see some getting ready to mate. They do a sort of dance with each other beforehand.

Spiders tend to spin their webs at night because it's safer to do so when most birds are asleep.

Penises!

SLIMY RING A RING O' ROSES

Fungi bloom on mild, damp nights. If you find one looking like this...

Come back in the morning and it'll be fully grown

WHERE DO ALL THE DIURNAL CREATURES GO?

Nighttime sounds totally different to daytime. Most creatures that buzz will be asleep, but listen out for chirping, especially if crickets live nearby.

Zzzzzz

I thought you were asleep?

Bees go back to their hives to sleep and keep warm.

Diurnal birds go to their roost. You might be able to figure out where this is from the guano (bird poop) underneath it.

Butterflies and flies find a nice spot away from predators and sheltered from any wild weather.

Often you notice things at night that you wouldn't spot during the day because all of your focus is on the small patch lit up by your light, with no distractions.

Moths and flies are attracted to light, so if you wear a headlamp, be prepared for flying insects to introduce themselves to your face. Best to keep your mouth closed.

ABSOLUTELY NO ADMITTANCE, I'M VEGETARIAN.

SOME GOOD WORDS TO KNOW

NOCTURNAL – Active during the nighttime
DIURNAL – Active during the daytime
CREPUSCULAR – Active at dawn and dusk
MATUTINAL – Active at dawn
VESPERTINE – Active at dusk

I can't go to school, I am vespertine.

PATIENCE

You might think that "patience" is just about the worst, most annoying word you've heard in your life. Having to be patient when you're waiting for a cake to be ready, or for someone to finish fixing your bike IS the worst and most annoying thing. But when it comes to observology, patience is the key if you want action, drama, tension and excitement. Take this spider's web as an example.

A SPIDER'S WEB	A FLY ARRIVES	IT GETS STUCK
Nice! It's a particularly elegant one.	Oh ho! Some action!	Looks like it's all over, red rover.
NO, WAIT!	IT FLIES STRAIGHT BACK INTO THE WEB	AH! HERE COMES THE SPIDER NOW
It wriggled free!	Well that was silly.	Is she going to reach the fly in time?
YES!	SHE'S DRAGGING THE FLY AWAY	
She injects her venom and swaddles the fly in silk.	She'll eat it in a safe hiding spot.	Fin.

HOW TO GET A FLY TO GO OUTSIDE (AT NIGHT)

Flies find light irresistibly attractive. You can use light to make a fly go exactly where you want it to.

A FLY

YOU (irritated)

Turn off the light in the room you want the fly to leave, open the door and turn on the light in the next room. Once the fly is in the next room, close the door so the fly can't return to the first room.

Do the same thing as many times as you need to, leading the fly closer and closer to the front door. It works best if you have an outside light too.

goodBYE

HIDING IN PLAIN SIGHT
some different types of camouflage

BLEND IN

Heehee, it can't see me!

LOOK LIKE SOMETHING BORING

A butterfly disguised as a dead leaf

A bird dropping spider disguised as poop

LOOK LIKE SOMETHING WONDERFUL

Oooh!

Orchid mantis mimicking a flower

A perfect baked potato costume

(Know what your quarry likes best)

COVER YOURSELF IN STUFF

Caddisfly larvae build protective cases out of bits and pieces they find

Some crabs grow seaweed on their back

"Home AND garden."

GIVE YOURSELF VERY THIN EDGES SO YOU WON'T MAKE A SHADOW

TOP VIEW

FRONT VIEW

ACTING NORMAL

INCOGNITO!

BE SEE-THROUGH

Jellyfish are particularly good at this

"Hee hee!"

47

Bare concrete might seem like a difficult place to find signs of life, but for someone who's paying attention there's plenty to look at. Tiny creatures can live in cracks and puddles, flying insects sunbathe on hot pavement and lichen happily grows anywhere. An observologist can do a spot of birdwatching here, even if the birds are nowhere to be seen.

PAVEMENT

ANTS

Fine wings like a queenly gown

QUEEN ANT

A crack in the pavement or a little gap at the bottom of a concrete wall is just the sort of place that an ant (and her 10,000 sisters) might live. Ants are always busy doing something, which makes them very interesting to observe. There's so much to learn about ants that the study of them gets a name of its own: myrmecology.

Ants belong to the order Hymenoptera, which includes wasps and bees. And like some of their Hymenoptera cousins, ants live in colonies. Other things they have in common:

Some species have a stinger for injecting venom

Their mouthparts have evolved to chomp and chew

Their larvae are quite maggotty in form

Gathers food

Looks after the eggs and young ants

Defends the nest

Every ant colony has at least one queen. She's the only one who can lay eggs. A queen ant is made when a larva is fed a particular diet. Newborn queens have wings so that they can fly away and start a new colony far from where they were born. Once they've settled down, they lose their wings and stay safely ensconced in their nest.

The ants you see out and about are female worker ants. They perform many different jobs to keep the colony running smoothly.

Male ants only have one job—leave the colony and find a queen to mate with!

KNOW YOUR ANTS!

Some ant species won't mind if you sit next to them and quietly watch what they're doing. Other kinds of ant will not tolerate it AT ALL and could give you a painful bite or a sting, such as the bull ant of Australia or the American bullet ant. So bear that in mind.

BLACK HOUSEHOLD ANT — tickles

BULL ANT — stings

A Typical Worker Ant

Ants are built a bit differently from most insects: instead of an abdomen and thorax, they have a mesosoma and a metasoma (or gaster).

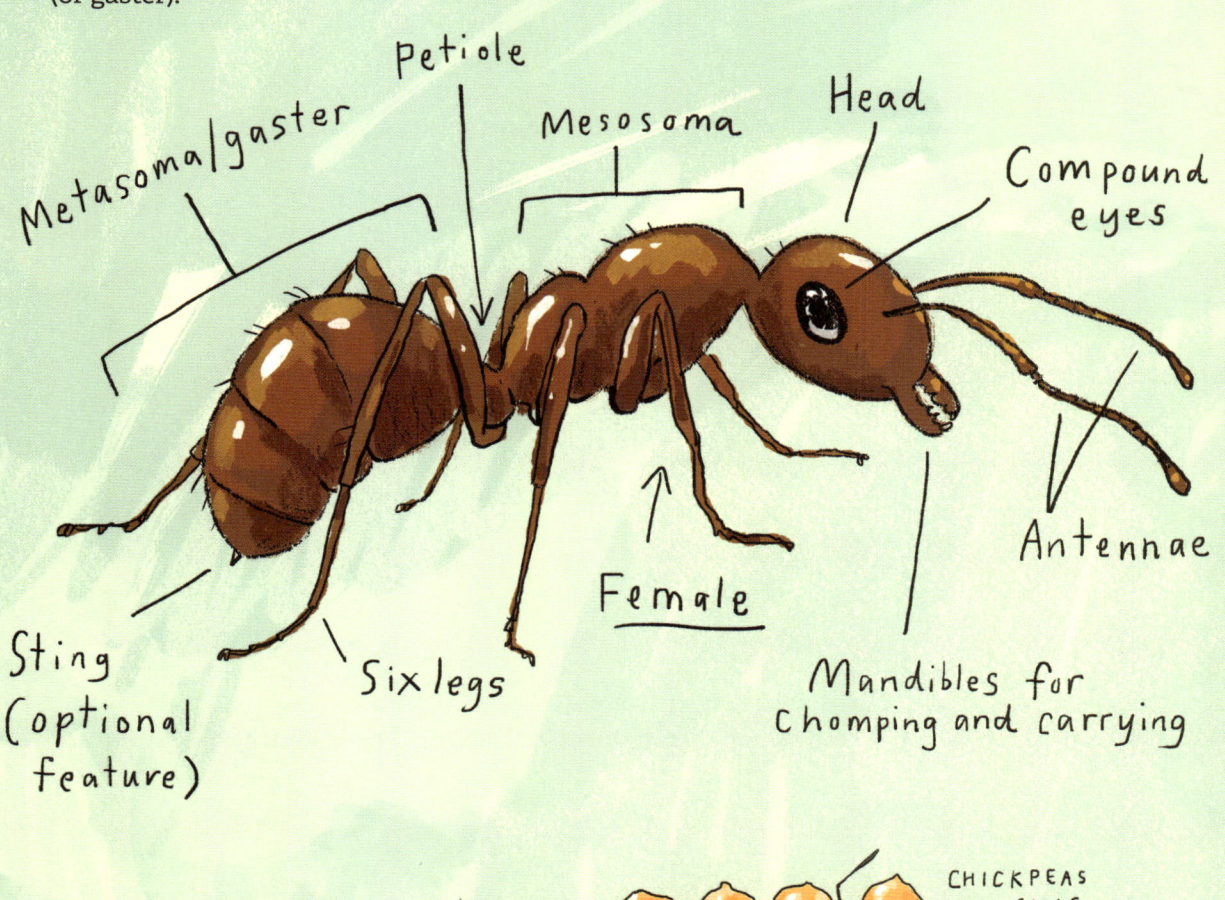

- Metasoma/gaster
- Petiole
- Mesosoma
- Head
- Compound eyes
- Antennae
- Female
- Mandibles for chomping and carrying
- Six legs
- Sting (optional feature)

Actual size of a Carebara bruni worker ant ↓

CHICKPEAS FOR SCALE

← Actual size of a worker ant from the Dinoponera genus

You can follow a highway of ants to find out where they're going and what they're doing.

51

If you disturb an ant nest there'll be an instant frenzy as the ants try to carry their eggs, larvae and pupae to safety.

Not shredded coconut, an ant's egg →

Oh! They're dismantling a large insect and taking it piece by piece back to their nest.

These ones are eating a bird poop. It seems like a strange choice for lunch but it must have some valuable nutrients in it.

When an ant finds something really great to eat, it makes a trail of smelly pheromones for other ants to follow and then pretty soon it's all hands on deck, ants galore! So a lone ant isn't necessarily lost. It might be a scout, on a bold quest to find new food for its colony.

If you see two ants pausing with their heads together, they're having a conversation. They use their antennae and their pheromones to communicate.

DO HUMANS COMMUNICATE WITH SMELLS TOO?

I DUNNO IF I WANT TO THINK ABOUT IT.

waft WAGGLE WAGGLE waft

If you see an ant outside, you could accidentally let a blob of jam slip out of your sandwich and onto the ground and then see what happens next.

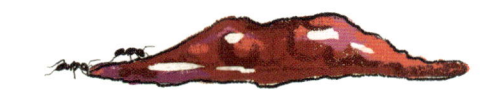

DUCK

GOOSE
(long, isn't it)

BLACKBIRD

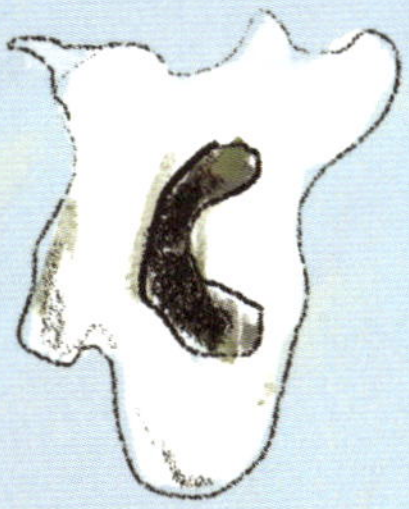

STARLING

BLACKBIRD WHO ATE A LOT OF PLUMS

CHICKEN

ROCK PIGEON

SPARROW

GULL

FROM THE OTHER END

Some birds vomit up things they can't digest in tidy pellets.

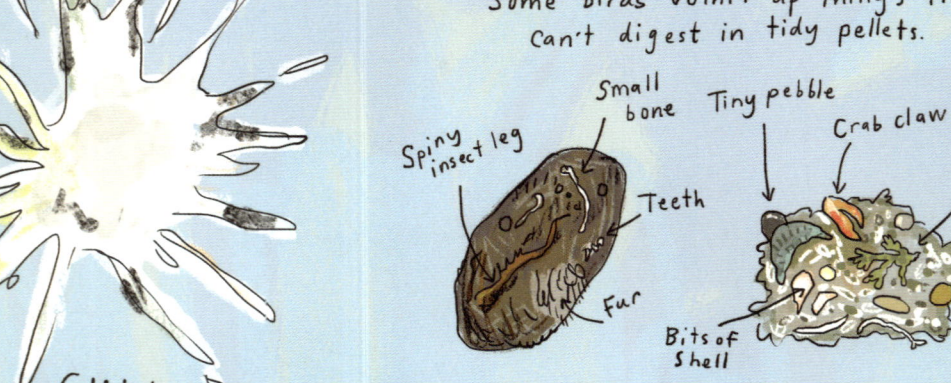

OWL PELLET — Spiny insect leg, Small bone, Teeth, Fur

GULL PELLET — Tiny pebble, Crab claw, Bristly seaweed, A hard seed, Bits of shell

BIRDWATCHING WITHOUT BIRDS

If you see a lot of guano (that's the word scientists use for bird poop) in one place on the ground, look up (carefully). This must be where birds often sit, roost or nest. This is probably not a good place to stand still for too long.

Birds have only one hole in their bottom and it's called a cloaca. They don't do separate poops and piddles; everything comes out together.

CLEVER CLOGS!

Multipurpose!

The "poop"
The "wee"

The hue and texture of bird poop depends on what the bird has been eating. If a bird has had a meal of purple or orange fruit, it will do purple or orange poop.

Seeds that will grow

WONDERFUL! EXCELLENT!

Some people believe that it's good luck to have a bird do a plop on you. It's nice to have a positive outlook on life.

COLLECTIONS

Collecting tiny things is brilliant because you can collect a LOT of things that won't take up much space, so no one can complain about your collection. An old matchbox or a little ointment jar will be perfect for housing your treasures.

SOME IDEAS FOR THINGS YOU MIGHT LIKE TO COLLECT

Nice pebbles

Tiny snail shell (uninhabited)

Fragment of a hatched bird's egg

An insect's wing

A pleasingly smooth seed

Feathers

Bright beetle wings that a spider has discarded from her web

A loose bit of lichen

Abandoned wasp nest

Dry leaves

The delicate shed skin of a spider

Finding a dead creature can be sad, but is also a rare opportunity. A living insect might be too fast or too dangerous to get a REALLY good look at, but when you find a dead one it's okay to poke and prod it.

You can tell a butterfly's had a long life and weathered many storms if its wings are dull and faded with raggedy holes and tatty edges. Feel how soft and furry its body is, and run your finger along its wings.

The wing of a dragonfly is a very special find. Because it's so big it's easy to see all the details.

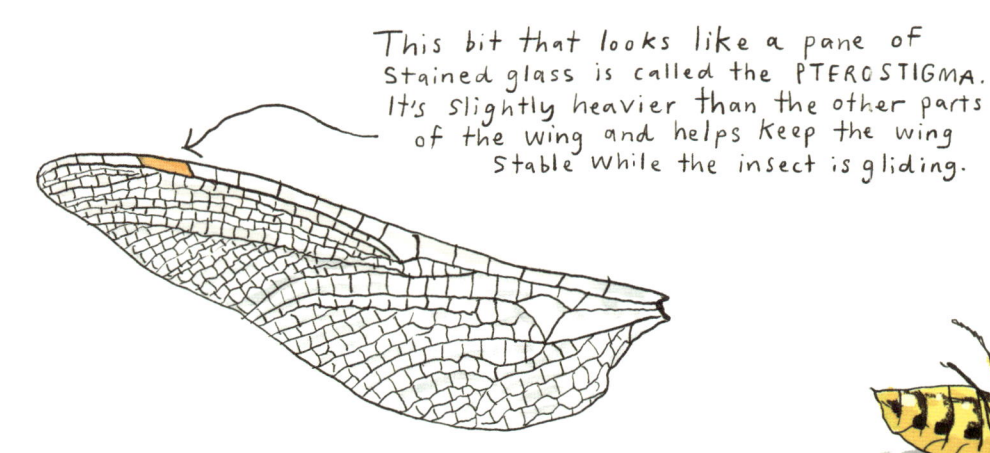

This bit that looks like a pane of stained glass is called the PTEROSTIGMA. It's slightly heavier than the other parts of the wing and helps keep the wing stable while the insect is gliding.

Take the time to study a dead wasp and you'll be better at spotting one that's buzzing around. Careful, though, a dead stinger can still sting!

Look closely at a dead insect and maybe you can tell why it died. Does it look squashed? Is it on the ground beneath a spider's web? Did it drown or get stuck inside something?

Check, too, that your "dead" animal is just that. It's a common tactic among beetles in particular to play dead to escape a threat. When an animal does this it's called thanatosis.

I'm not dead. I'm just pretending until you leave me alone.

This praying mantis lost a fight against a wasp.

57

LICHEN

Lichen (sounds like *liken*) is EVERYWHERE. It's quite common to see it growing on concrete paths or walls. It's strange and wonderful and always worth a closer look.

A lichen is what happens when two kinds of fungi join up with algae (or bacteria) and together they grow into something they could never be on their own. It's not a plant, it's not algae, it's not a fungus…it's a lichen!

They can grow just about anywhere, from the middle of the desert to Antarctica. They'll grow on almost anything that stays still for long enough. Trees, rocks, metal roofs, plastic things, fences, cliffs, old bones. However they grow VERY slowly, sometimes only by a hair's breadth each year.

SOME CATEGORIES of LICHEN

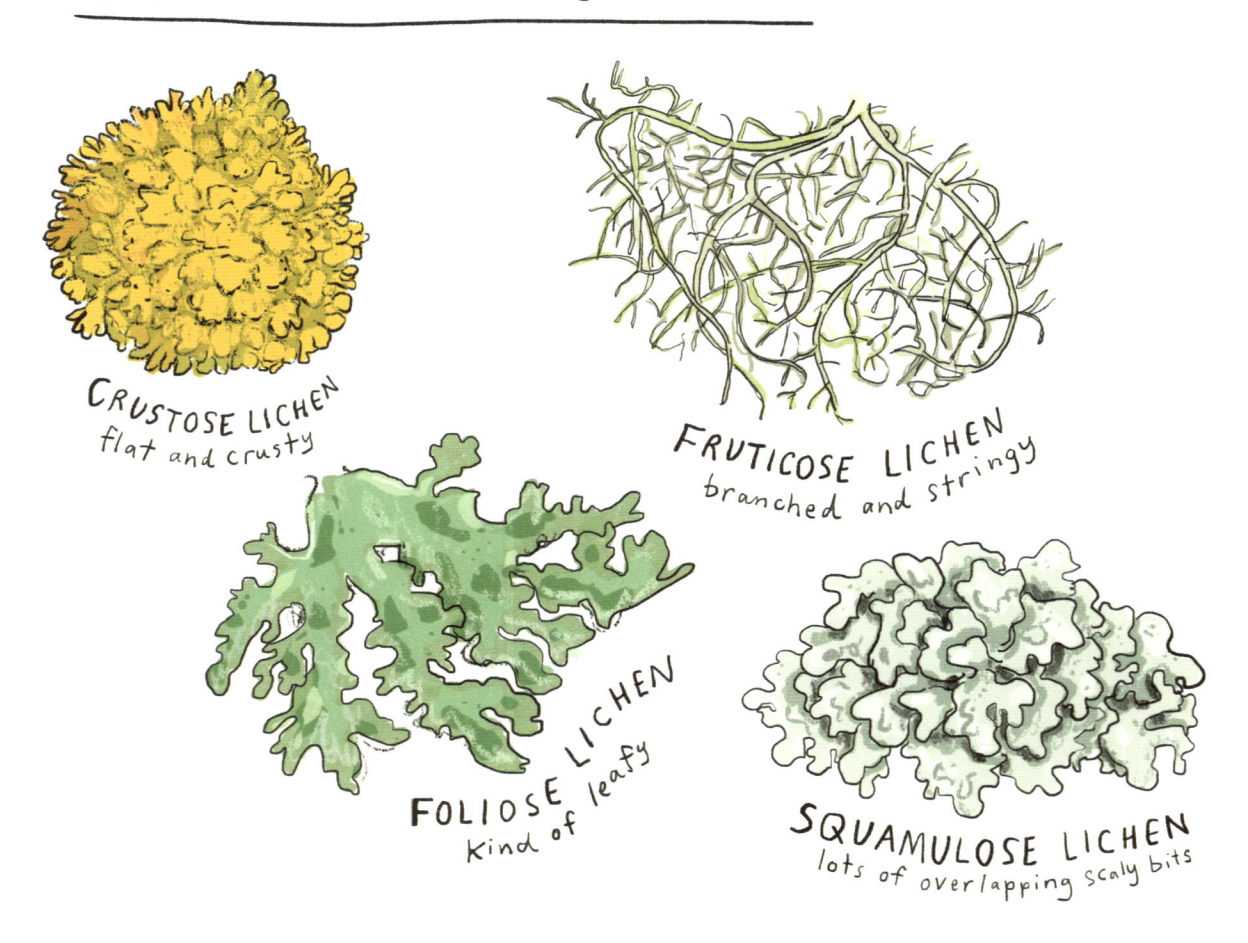

CRUSTOSE LICHEN — flat and crusty

FRUTICOSE LICHEN — branched and stringy

FOLIOSE LICHEN — kind of leafy

SQUAMULOSE LICHEN — lots of overlapping scaly bits

Lichen can be as peculiar and alien-looking as anything you might find growing on a tropical reef. When it's time for them to reproduce they grow special structures for releasing spores. Some look like pinheads, or bugles for fairies.

These magical growths are only about 1cm tall, so look VERY closely.

THIS IS A TARDIGRADE →

A tardigrade is a very cute microscopic animal that's often found living on lichens. Your average tardigrade is about the size of the dot on this i, and yet it has the things bigger animals have, like a brain and a digestive system. Remarkable!

To a tardigrade, a lichen would seem like a great, rolling landscape. That's something nice to think about when you next see one.

Non-scientifically known as a water bear or moss piglet

PHENOLOGY

> Tuesday 22nd — Today my pet spider's eggs hatched. Now I have 128 pet spiders.

Phenology is the observation of seasonal patterns in nature. A phenologist pays attention to animal habits, plant growth and weather, and makes a note of what they see every day.

If you get into the habit of phenologizing, after a few years you'll have an amazing record of the yearly cycles taking place around you. You might even start seeing patterns. Do the plum blossoms come out a little bit earlier each year? Is there a species of moth that only shows up on your windows every second year?

You don't have to focus on everything all at once. If you try and monitor EVERYTHING it'll be an overwhelming job that might not be fun for long. A good way to start would be to concentrate on just a few of the things you like best, and make a short note in your diary when something significant happens.

SOME SUGGESTIONS to GET YOU STARTED

If there's a hedge with lovely fragrant flowers that you walk past every day on the way to school, write down when you first get a wonderful whiff from it.

A deciduous tree changes a lot during the year. You can observe: when its leaves first turn from green to brown, when the last leaf has fallen to the ground, when its branches grow tiny buds, and when its first new green leaf appears. (Deciduous trees lose their leaves in the colder months, whereas evergreens keep their foliage all year round.)

Tiny nub where a new leaf will sprout from

A YEAR of SPARROWS

Sparrows may seem like everyday birds, but the longer you watch them, and spot their habits, the more interesting they become. For instance, when it's time for them to find a mate you might hear a lot of fussing and fighting. When they're building a nest, you can watch them gather material for it. They act differently in hot and cold weather, and they eat different things at different times of the year too.

Puff themselves up to stay warm on cold days

Make little dips in the dust to clean themselves when it's dry

Collect long pieces of dry grass to make their nest with

Their wingbeats sound different when they're carrying something

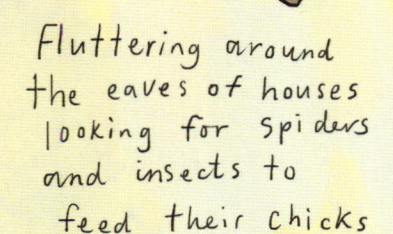

Fluttering around the eaves of houses looking for spiders and insects to feed their chicks

A lot of squabbling over mates or territory

A DIRECTORY of DROPPINGS

SLUG or SNAIL

EARTHWORM

HONEY BEE

COCKROACH

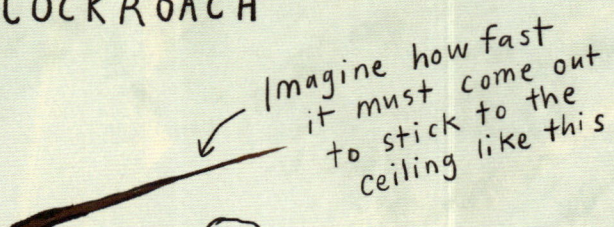

Imagine how fast it must come out to stick to the ceiling like this

OR

SPIDER

↑ Flat white spots

HOUSE FLY

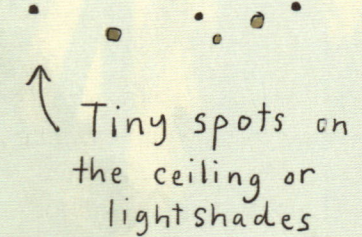

↑ Tiny spots on the ceiling or light shades

CATERPILLAR

Chunky, dry insect poops like these can be called FRASS

The first thing a BUTTERFLY does after it emerges from its chrysalis is a sloppy red poop.

EGG EXAMPLES

EARTHWORM

SLUG or SNAIL
Translucent little pearls

BUTTERFLY
Underside of a leaf

MOTH
or maybe

SPIDER

ANT

COCKROACH

PRAYING MANTIS
Each cell contains an individual egg

HOUSE FLY

A nice word to know: ovum is Latin for "egg" (the plural is ova) and it's where the word "oval" comes from. Admittedly, there aren't many oval ova on this page.

Females of some insects have one of these. It looks like a stinger, but on non-stinging species like this cricket it's harmless. It's an ovipositor—literally an egg depositor! She can poke it into the soil to lay her eggs safely below the surface.

WORMS

Worms are wonderful. Even though they mostly live underground, it's surprising how often you'll see them up on top. Worms belong to the phylum Annelida, which has thousands of species.

In 1979 Swedish scientists found evidence that earthworms can feel pleasure and pain. Isn't it strange that we assumed they didn't? But it's a good reason to be kind to them.

If you pick up a worm it'll try to squeeze between your fingers because it thinks they're something to burrow under. It's best not to handle a worm for too long because hands tend to be warm and dry, the exact opposite of what a worm enjoys.

What seems like a short worm can be surprisingly long when it stretches itself out.

THESE ETERNAL PLAINS... AM I HALLUCINATING?

A worm who is going places

When it rains, worms feel the vibrations of the raindrops hitting the ground and they come to the surface. They can move much more quickly over wet ground than they can underground (when it's sunny, they're likely to dry out). It's an efficient way to travel if they're looking for food, new habitats or friends.

That's why you see so many worms trying to cross roads and tennis courts on rainy days. Sometimes they get stuck in puddles and need help getting out before they drown. If they look soft and milky, you've arrived too late, unfortunately.

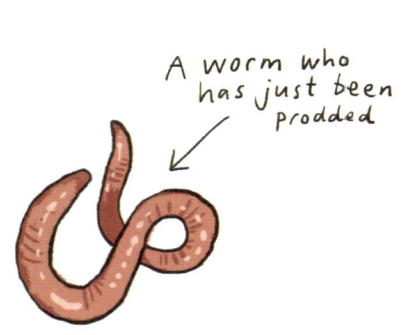

A worm who has just been prodded

A WORM THAT GOT TOO WET

A WORM THAT GOT TOO DRY

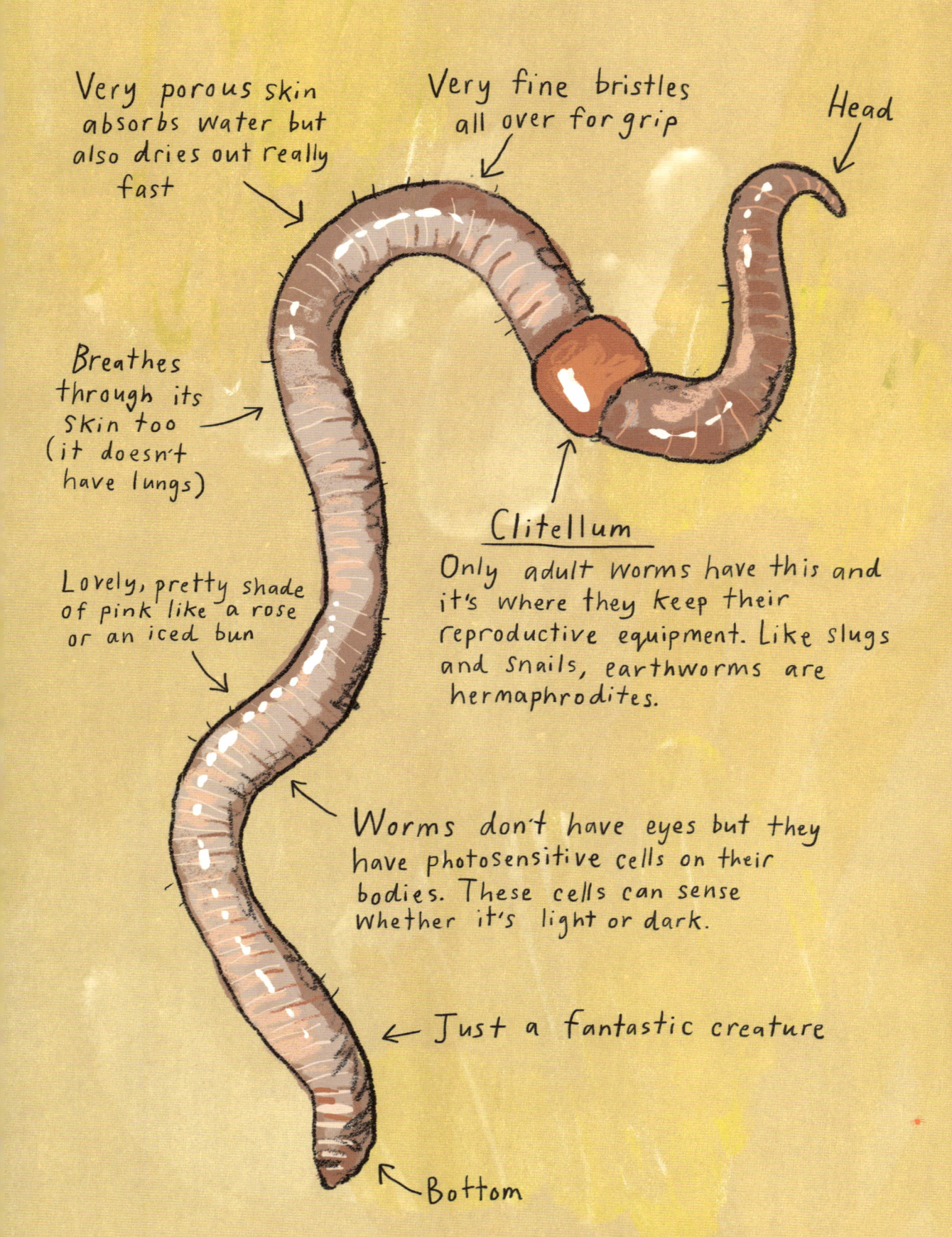

Very porous skin absorbs water but also dries out really fast

Very fine bristles all over for grip

Head

Breathes through its skin too (it doesn't have lungs)

Lovely, pretty shade of pink like a rose or an iced bun

Clitellum
Only adult worms have this and it's where they keep their reproductive equipment. Like slugs and snails, earthworms are hermaphrodites.

Worms don't have eyes but they have photosensitive cells on their bodies. These cells can sense whether it's light or dark.

← Just a fantastic creature

← Bottom

VERMICAST ↗

Have you ever sat on a patch of grass and noticed little knobbly piles of dirt, like tiny bunches of grapes made of mud? That's worm poop; it's called vermicast.

Earthworms lay cocoons (different to the kind moths make) and each one can have many eggs inside it. These *Lumbricus terrestris* cocoons look like teeny-weeny lemons.

Worms differ in habits from one species to another. The tiger worms in your compost bin or worm farm like to munch on decaying food scraps and manure. The common earthworm eats dead leaves and soil as it burrows through your lawn.

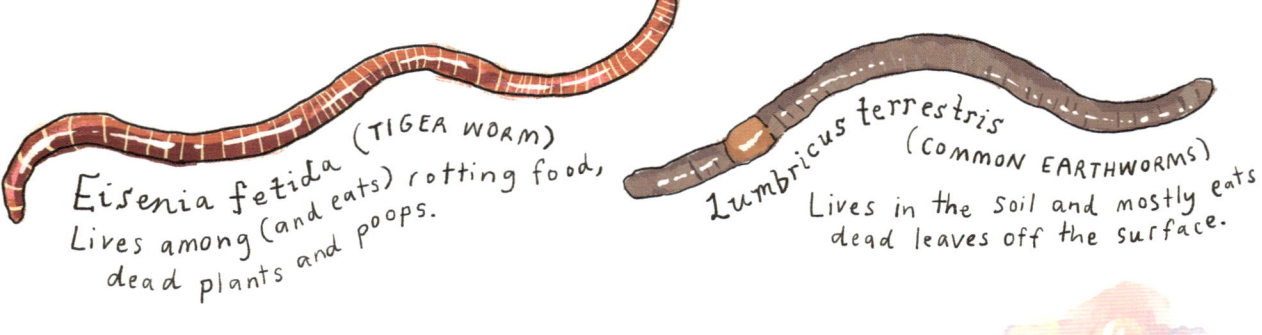

↙ EARTHWORM COCOONS

Eisenia fetida (TIGER WORM)
Lives among (and eats) rotting food, dead plants and poops.

Lumbricus terrestris (COMMON EARTHWORMS)
Lives in the soil and mostly eats dead leaves off the surface.

Some earthworms have an opalescent sheen to them. Opalescence looks like this ↗

HOW TO CATCH WORMS LIKE A BIRD

Tapping and scratching on the ground can bring worms to the surface.

1. Drum your feet on the ground.

2. Pause to listen and look for movement. Repeat step one if you need to.

3. When a worm approaches the surface, plunge your beak in and gobble it up.

THUMPA THUMPA THUMP

HUH?

OH NO

OH YES

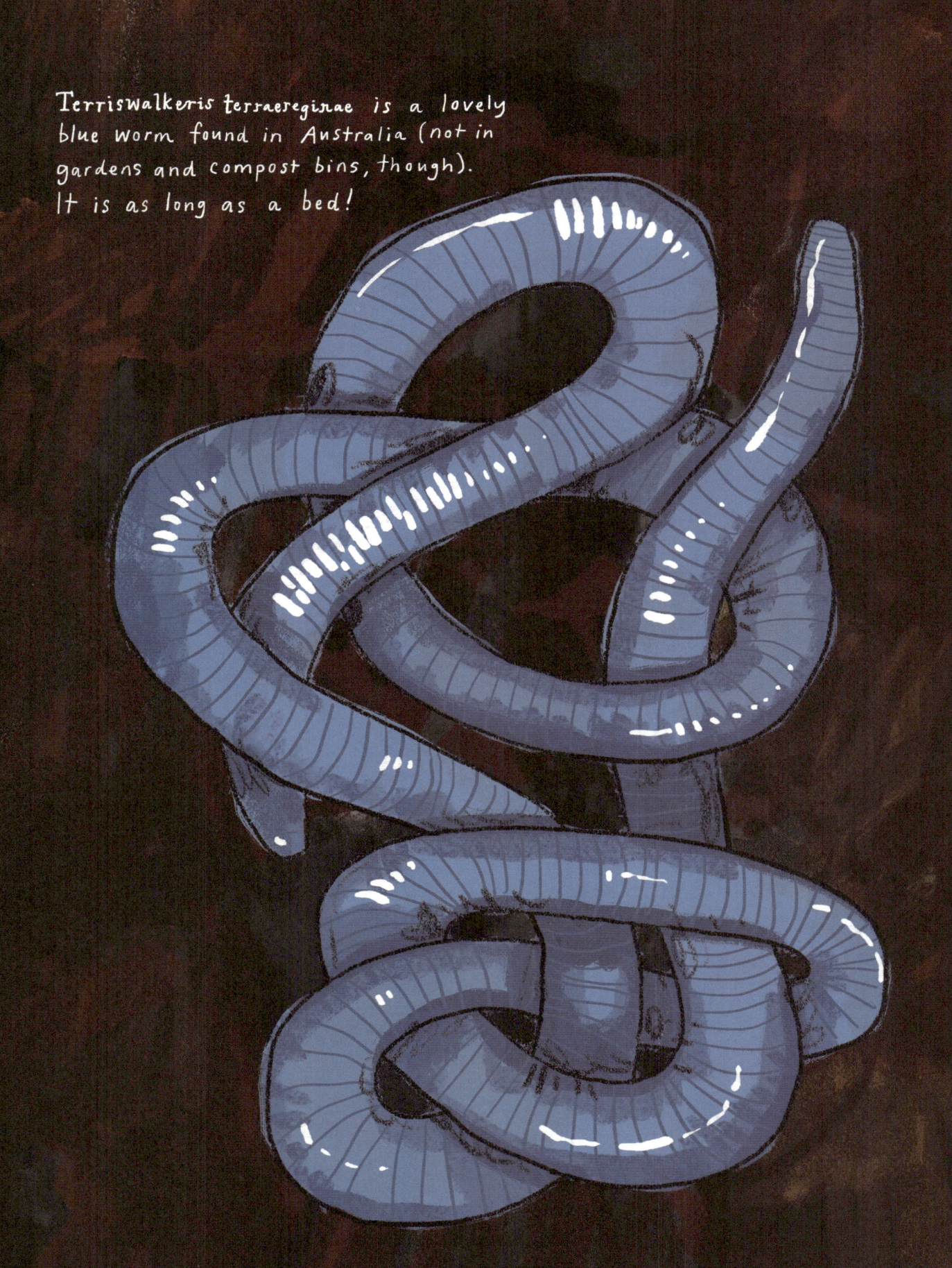

Terriswalkeris terraereginae is a lovely blue worm found in Australia (not in gardens and compost bins, though). It is as long as a bed!

HOW TO SAVE A WORM THAT'S IN DANGER OF BEING STOMPED ON

DON'T pick up a worm between your fingers like this. It's too easy to squish it.

Ooooof!

Instead, try to gently scoop it onto something flat like a leaf.

Carry it on the palm of your hand to a patch of nice loose dirt and let it go. Make sure it's in the shade. Well done!

Away you go, mate

HOW TO SNEAK UP ON A BUG

Some creatures, like caterpillars and beetles, won't be bothered by you watching them closely, but others, like frogs and grasshoppers, are easily spooked away.

Is it true? Someone is admiring moi??

THIS SEEMS OMINOUS

If it's a sunny day take care not to let your shadow pass over the creature you're stalking. They'll notice the change in light and fly, jump or scuttle away.

Keep your breath steady. If you blow a puff of air onto a creature it'll get a fright.

(Incidentally, if there's a bug crawling on you and you don't want it to, a quick puff of air is a good way to gently remove it.)

Think slug thoughts, think slug thoughts...

Mmm... decomposing plants...

Move as gracefully as a slug, approaching your target as slowly as you can. Do this and you'll be an expert creeper-upper in no time.

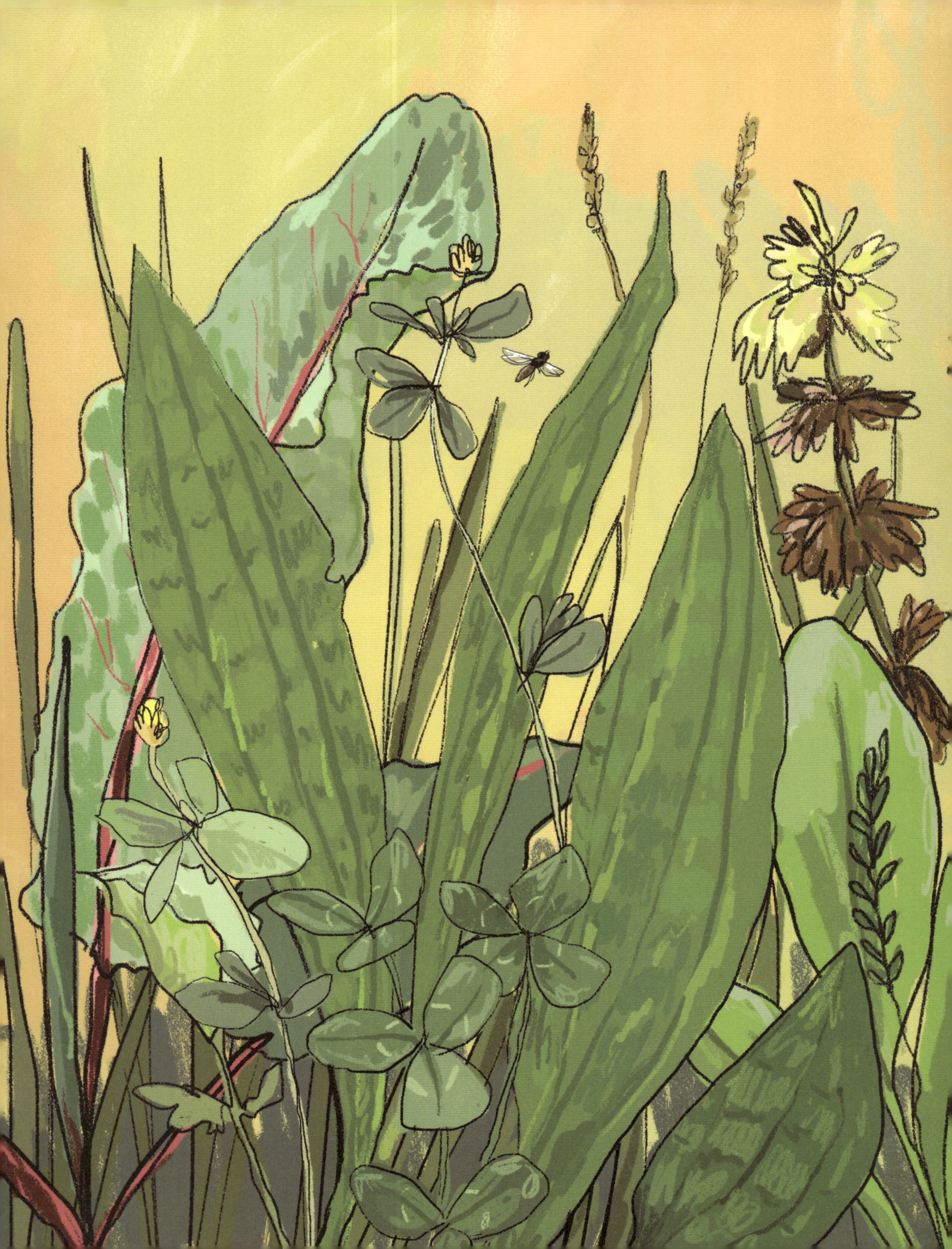

A WEEDY PATCH

An observologist knows that where plants grow, creatures will follow. Gardens, parks, hedges and slightly unkempt lawns are all excellent habitats. Flowers will attract pollinators like bees, flies and moths, which in turn provide a buffet for spiders. Fallen leaves are a feast for slaters, millipedes and worms—which in turn are a feast for birds!

Honey bees accumulating dusty pollen from flowers; it's used to feed baby bees.

BEES

Honey bees and bumblebees are the types of bee you're most likely to encounter. Happily, they're small but not microscopic so we can easily see what they're doing. See if you can spot a bee cleaning herself. She'll use her legs to comb her hair in a way that's almost catlike.

If you let a bee mind her own business and you're not disturbing her hive, she's very unlikely to sting you, so there's no need to be afraid when you see one.

This one is a charming little mason bee.

SOME HONEY BEE BUSINESS

Slurping nectar for energy and honey production. Honey is their winter food supply.

See if you can spot a bee's little tongue

Collecting water to take back to the hive for humidity control—successfully storing honey requires a lot of hard work and precisely the right atmosphere.

Damp moss

People keep honey bees in hand-built hives all over the world, so they're not wild animals. But you can't put a leash on a bee, let alone 50,000 bees from one hive. Luckily, they're nice to have around. The scientific name for honey bees is *Apis mellifera*, meaning "bee that bears honey".

Honey bee drones (males) have one purpose: to mate with a queen bee so she'll lay eggs. Mating can be over quite quickly. The honey bees that you see on flowers are all females.

A HONEY BEE DRONE

I'm a highly focused individual.

Eyes so big they basically touch in the middle

If a bumblebee lifts its middle leg it means "LEAVE ME ALONE!"

When you see a bee attending to flowers, look for her pollen baskets. There's a hairy spot on a bee's back legs that holds all the pollen she gathers until it can be dropped off back at the hive. Pollen isn't always yellow, so depending on which flowers she has visited, the little blob the bee carries can be white, orange, red or even blue.

Look at all that pollen! EMPLOYEE OF THE MONTH!!

Honey bees and bumblebees are very well-known to us, but you could often be looking at a bee and not know it. There are myriad ways to be a bee. It's always good to remember just how many wildly different species exist in the world and not get too hung up on what we're familiar with.

Doesn't live in a hive

I hate group projects.

Leioproctus paahaumaa
SOLITARY BEE
(New Zealand)

Not yellow, no stripes!

Augochlora pura
PURE GREEN SWEAT BEE
(North America)

Very tiny and doesn't sting

Tetragonula carbonaria
STINGLESS BEE
(Australia)

VULTURE BEES

Some bees go so firmly against bee stereotypes that most people would be shocked to know that they exist! Vulture bees live in Central America.

It would be a stinky world without some of us to clean up the dead stuff.

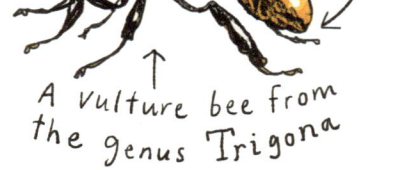

No sting!

Instead of visiting flowers, vulture bees visit dead animals to collect **MEAT**.

A vulture bee from the genus Trigona

HOW TO HELP AN EXHAUSTED HONEY BEE or BUMBLEBEE

If it's a particularly chilly day, or if a bee didn't make it back to her hive before bedtime, she'll be cold and exhausted. Sometimes all she needs is a sugary snack to get her going again, and you can give her that.

In a very shallow saucer (the lid of a jar is good) mix sugar with just enough cold water to make it syrupy. Don't use honey because unfortunately that could spread a serious bee disease.

Madame.

Put it as close to the bee as you can.

What's this then?

Fingers crossed, the bee will smell it and have a nice big drink. You might have to be quite patient at this point; she might not move very quickly.

So long!

With a bit of luck, after a few minutes she'll be feeling much better and will fly away. If not, it could just be time for that bee to die.

DIFFERENT BEES BUILD DIFFERENT HOMES

I tried knitting sweaters but my larvae don't have arms so they kept slipping off.

WOOL CARDER BEE

Gathers fine furry tufts from plants and uses them to construct cells to lay eggs in.

A drill?! That would be cheating.

CARPENTER BEE

Chews a tunnel in a piece of wood and lays its eggs in there.

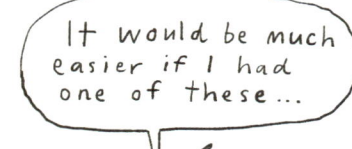

PLASTERER BEE

Lines each cell of its nest with a smooth coating that it secretes from its mouth.

It would be much easier if I had one of these...

DIGGER BEE

Makes its nest by digging a hole in the ground.

LEAF-CUTTER BEE

Chews off neat circular bits of leaves and uses them to build its hive.

NOTE: Many species fall into each of these categories!

COMMON WASP vs HONEY BEE

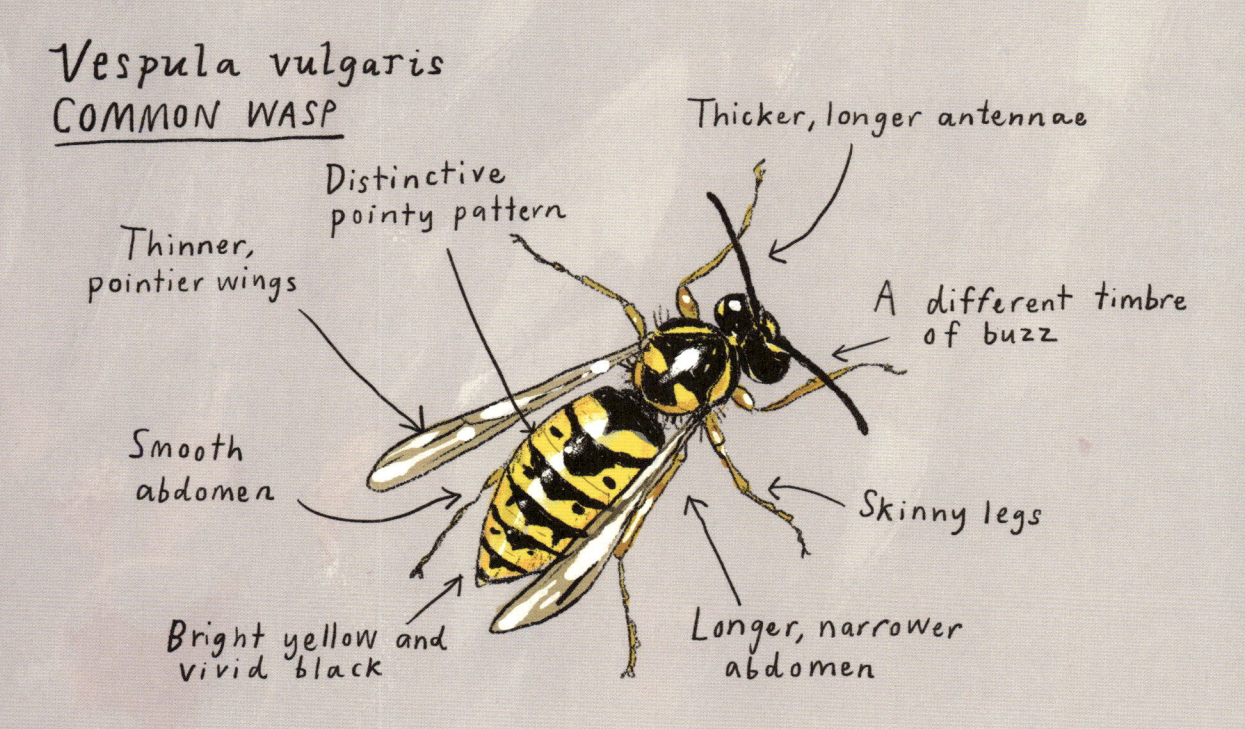

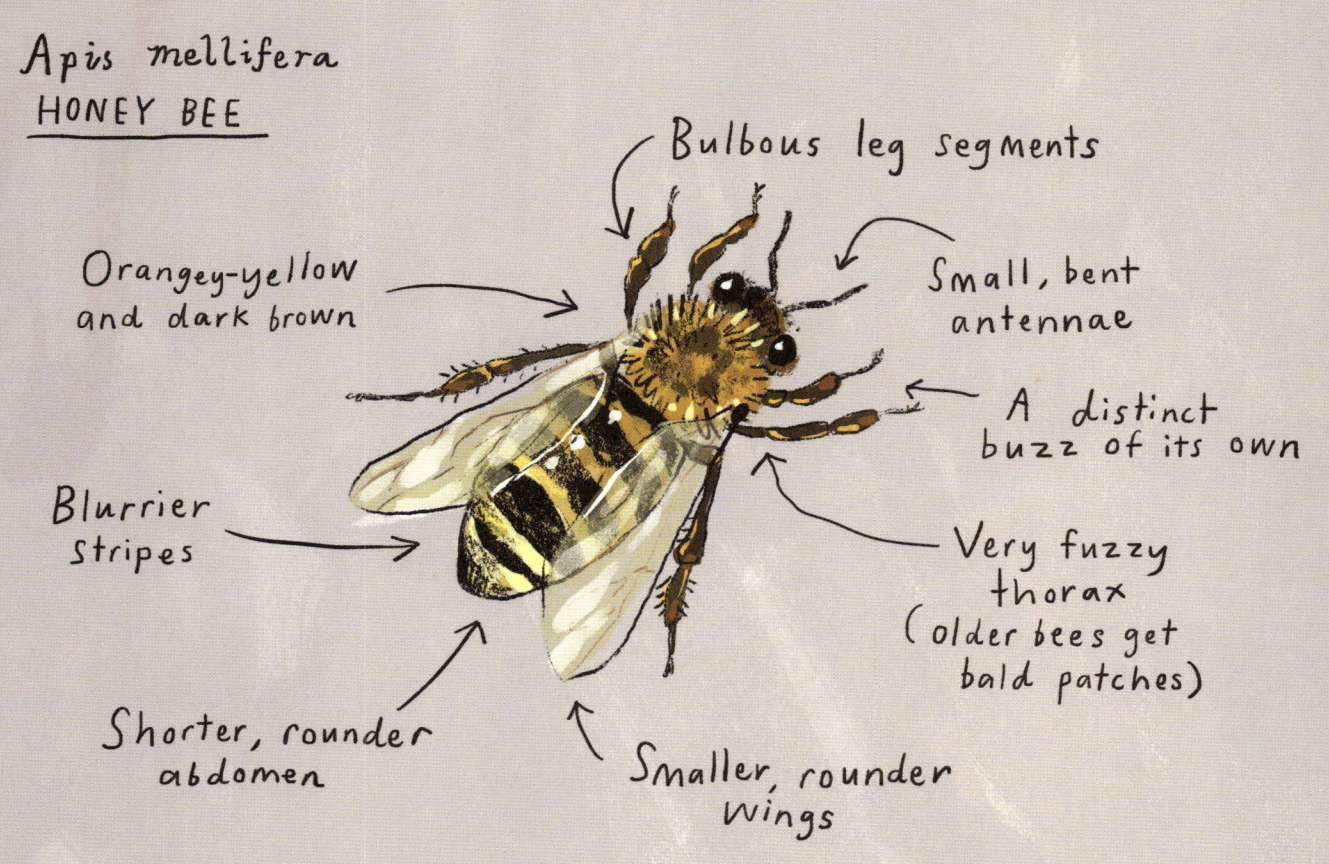

Vespula vulgaris
COMMON WASP

- Thicker, longer antennae
- Distinctive pointy pattern
- Thinner, pointier wings
- A different timbre of buzz
- Smooth abdomen
- Skinny legs
- Bright yellow and vivid black
- Longer, narrower abdomen

Apis mellifera
HONEY BEE

- Bulbous leg segments
- Orangey-yellow and dark brown
- Small, bent antennae
- A distinct buzz of its own
- Blurrier stripes
- Very fuzzy thorax (older bees get bald patches)
- Shorter, rounder abdomen
- Smaller, rounder wings

WASPS

I'm hunting spiders... What page are they on?

Wasps have a reputation for being like the honey bee's evil twin. This isn't really fair. There are thousands of wasp species and many of them are important pollinators and pest controllers. Some are very beautiful.

The species we're most familiar with is *Vespula vulgaris*, the big yellow one that makes a nuisance of itself at picnics, buzzing around your jam sandwich.

Common wasps are really only a problem where humans have introduced them to places they don't naturally belong, like New Zealand, where they don't have any predators so the population can grow very fast and they eat more than their share!

Their diet includes big fat caterpillars and unsuspecting spiders. They love overripe fruit too, and will steal honey from beehives if they can. They're very resourceful.

A number of wasps, including common, German and paper wasps, make incredible nests by chewing timber and mixing it with saliva into a fine pulp. They use this to build a structure that looks like it's made of delicate paper. You'll want to be completely sure that a nest is abandoned before you admire it though.

A COMMON WASP NEST

Wasp colonies have one queen, just as honey bees do. In spring, young queens fly around looking for a good place to start a new colony. You'll know when you see one because they're about twice the size of a worker wasp!

I need a big head to hold my big crown.

A FEW OTHER WASPS TO CONSIDER

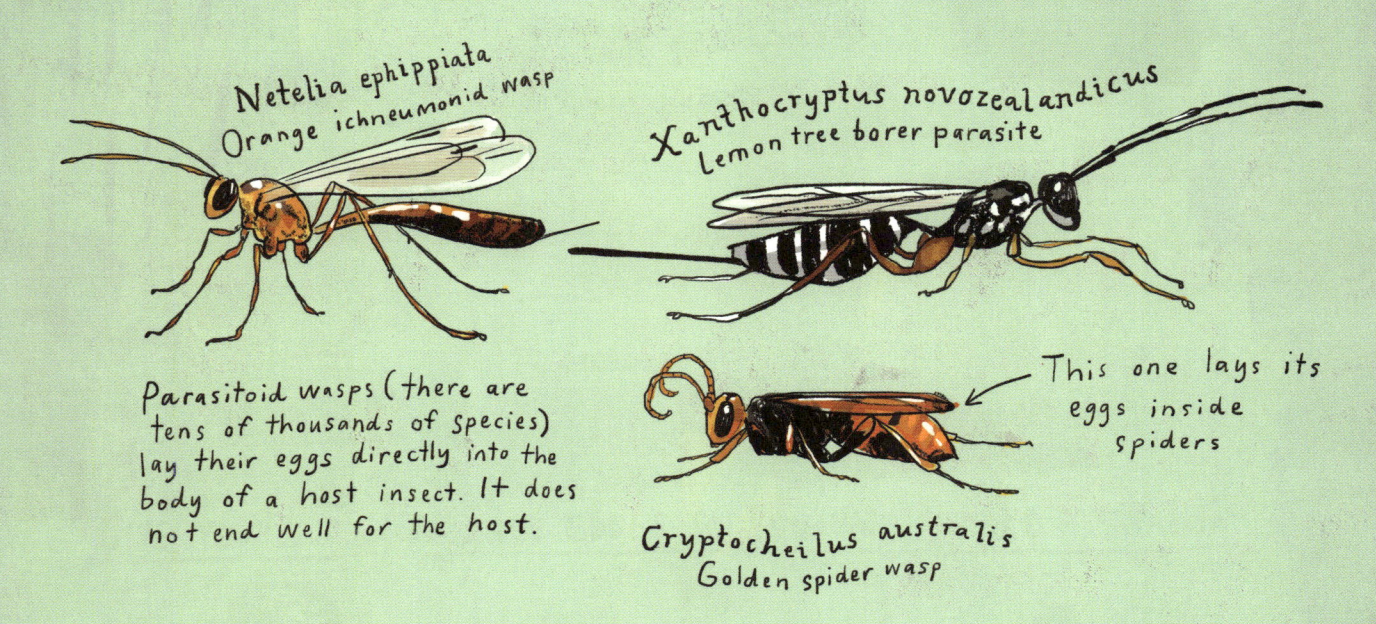

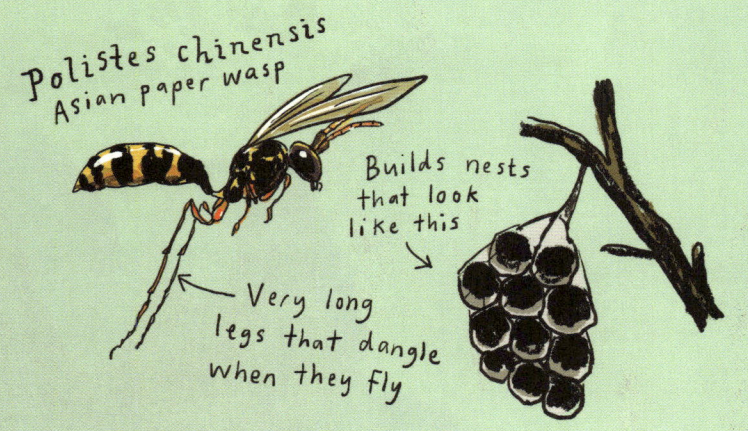

Netelia ephippiata
Orange ichneumonid wasp

Xanthocryptus novozealandicus
Lemon tree borer parasite

Parasitoid wasps (there are tens of thousands of species) lay their eggs directly into the body of a host insect. It does not end well for the host.

This one lays its eggs inside spiders

Cryptocheilus australis
Golden spider wasp

Polistes chinensis
Asian paper wasp

Builds nests that look like this

Very long legs that dangle when they fly

If you're observing monarch butterfly caterpillars and they keep disappearing, one of these wasps might be feeding them to her larvae.

less than 2mm

Ceratosolen capensis
Fig wasp

Wasps are pollinators too. This minuscule wasp pollinates fig trees.

Chrysura refulgens
Cuckoo wasp

This is a gloriously vibrant cuckoo wasp. It lays its eggs in the nest of another insect and then the young wasps eat the eggs or larvae of the host.

THINGS TO FIDDLE WITH

CICADA NYMPH BROOCH

When a cicada nymph (sounds like *nimf*). is ready to become an adult, it crawls out of the ground and sheds its skin. You'll find the empty skins stuck to trees and fences; they're very delicate! You can gently pick one up and hook it onto your clothing like a fancy brooch.

WHOMPH

WHOMPH

WHOMPH

(You have to make your own sound effects, sorry)

SYCAMORE SEED PROPELLER

Toss a sycamore seed into the air and watch it spin gently to the ground like the blade of a helicopter.

ROSE THORN RHINO HORN

Try not to prick yourself, but if you carefully pry a big thorn off a rose bush you can press the flat side against your nose and it'll stay there. Instant rhinoceros disguise!

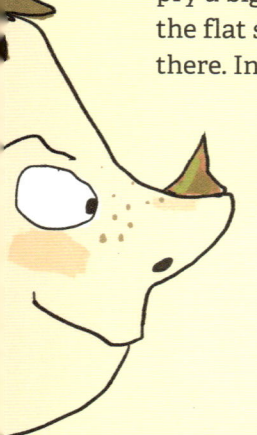

Do I know you from somewhere?

PLANTAIN PEA SHOOTER

Plantain is a common weed and its flower heads make excellent projectiles. It's pretty gentle but don't aim it at people or animals—that's mean.

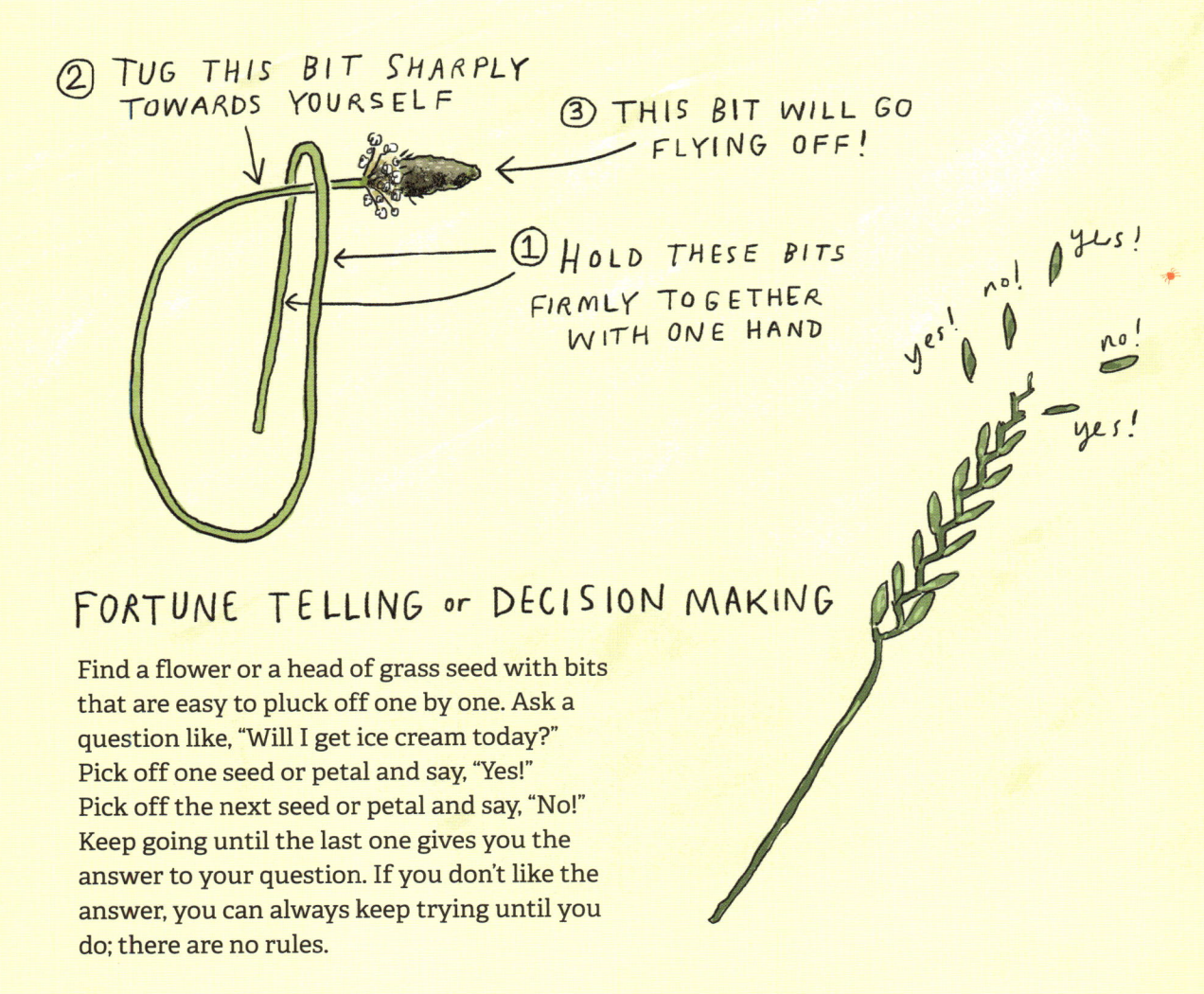

② TUG THIS BIT SHARPLY TOWARDS YOURSELF

③ THIS BIT WILL GO FLYING OFF!

① HOLD THESE BITS FIRMLY TOGETHER WITH ONE HAND

FORTUNE TELLING or DECISION MAKING

Find a flower or a head of grass seed with bits that are easy to pluck off one by one. Ask a question like, "Will I get ice cream today?" Pick off one seed or petal and say, "Yes!" Pick off the next seed or petal and say, "No!" Keep going until the last one gives you the answer to your question. If you don't like the answer, you can always keep trying until you do; there are no rules.

A FAIRY'S TOOTHBRUSH

Inside a periwinkle flower is a fairy's toothbrush. You can carefully remove the petals one by one to find it. Fairies must have very clean teeth.

IT LOOKS LIKE THIS BUT SMALLER

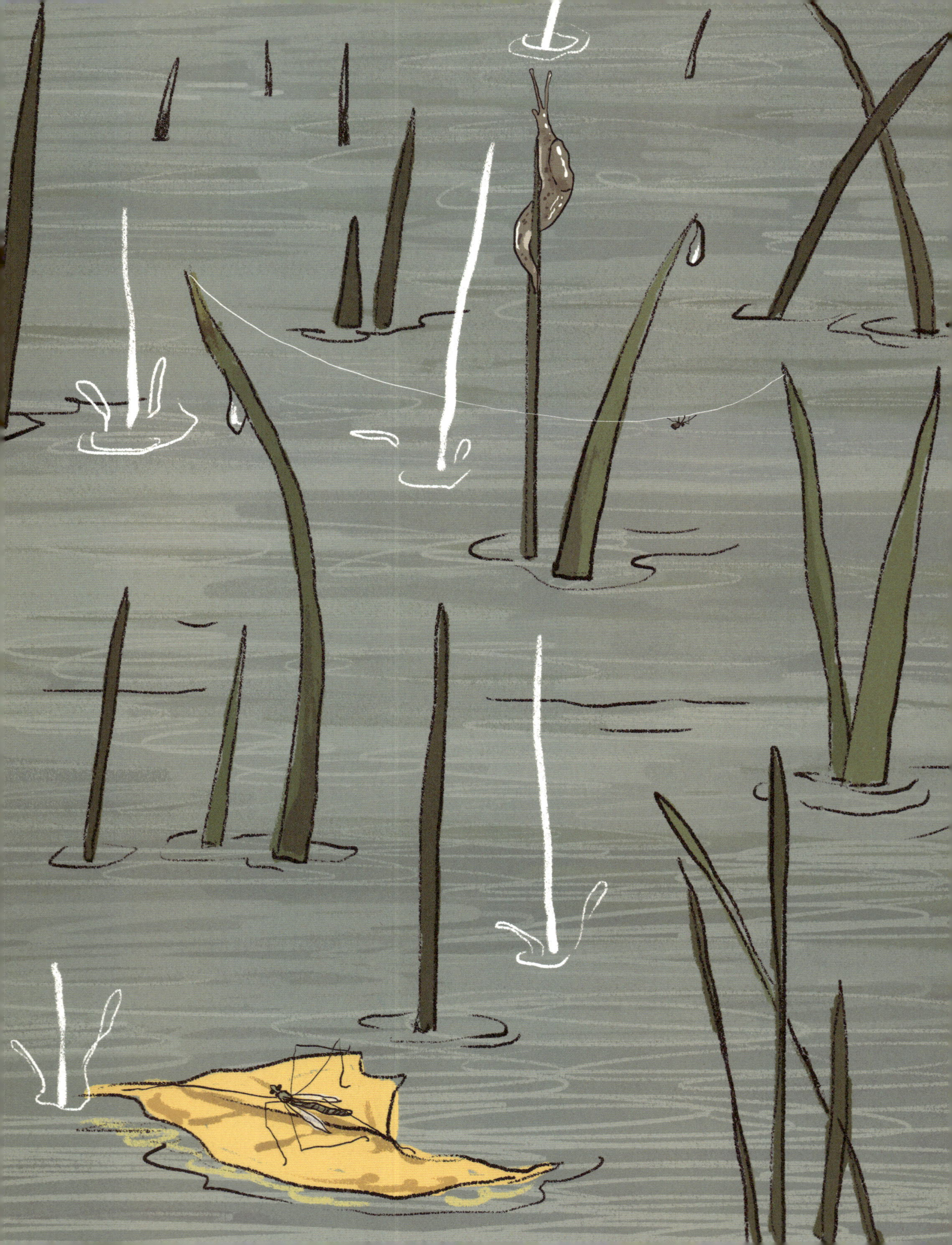

WET DAYS

Sorry! Bye!

When it rains so much that a lawn turns into one enormous puddle, the animals that live in the grass climb to the tip of each blade and hope that the water won't come any higher.

Tiny spiders can make an escape by casting a silk thread into the air and letting it carry them away like a kite.

Slugs and snails like to be wet, but they'll drown in too much water.

Some creatures are so small, they can walk on the surface of water without sinking.

This isn't fair! I'm supposed to get my wings next week!

Tentacles crossed for good luck

TIP TOE TIP TOE

SURFACE TENSION

Surface tension is like an invisible skin that holds water together. It's what makes a drop of water sit upright and it's why a bellyflop hurts so much.

If you take a full cup of water, then keep adding to it drop by drop, you'll see that you can actually fill the cup ABOVE the brim. This is because surface tension is holding the water in place; it's amazing!

Say when.

A big animal like you can break the surface tension of water without even noticing, but if you're the size of an ant it's not so easy. Imagine being so small that you could drown inside a raindrop.

Growing Up as an Insect

Some species change so much over the course of their lifetime, you'd be forgiven for thinking they were two completely different creatures.

Growing up as a human isn't all smooth sailing either, but when you get to adulthood all your body parts will be in pretty much the same place as they started. And you'll still have a mouth, which is more than some adult moths can say.

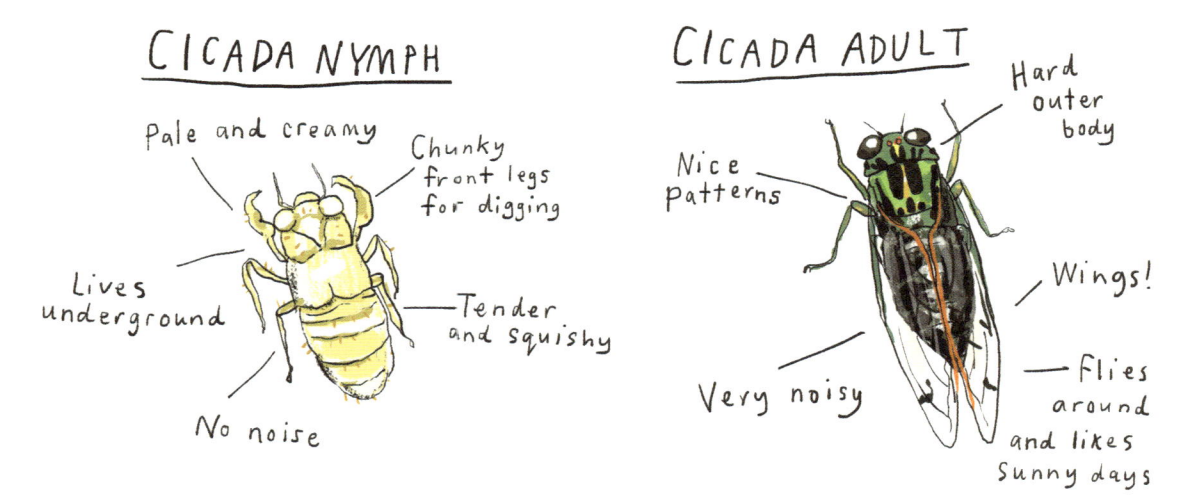

CICADA NYMPH

- Pale and creamy
- Chunky front legs for digging
- Lives underground
- Tender and squishy
- No noise

CICADA ADULT

- Hard outer body
- Nice patterns
- Wings!
- Flies around and likes sunny days
- Very noisy

Some insects have three phases to their life. They begin as an egg, which then hatches as a nymph; then, when the nymph is big enough, it sheds its skin to reveal its adult form.

Other insects have four phases to their life: egg, larva, pupa, adult.

The pupal stage is when the larva has eaten and grown enough to become an adult but needs to undergo HUGE changes before that can happen. It stops eating and forms a kind of protective shell in which to undergo its transformation. Chrysalises and cocoons are examples of pupae.

A BEETLE PUPATING

Looks kind of like a beetle-shaped gummy bear

Of course, not everything changes so dramatically as it grows up. This praying mantis nymph just looks like a tiny praying mantis. →

LARVAL LANGUAGE

A maggot is a blowfly larva

Grubs are beetle larvae

A caterpillar is the larva of a moth or butterfly

You were a very grubby baby.

CHRYSALIS

A chrysalis doesn't have a butterfly inside it; it IS the butterfly.

To form a chrysalis a caterpillar attaches itself with silk to a plant, building or fence and then sheds its skin so it no longer looks like a caterpillar. Its legs fall off and so does its head! Inside this new headless skin, the caterpillar's body reconfigures into a butterfly.

When it's ready, it sheds the outer skin once more and—ta da! Now it's a butterfly!

CABBAGE WHITE BUTTERFLY

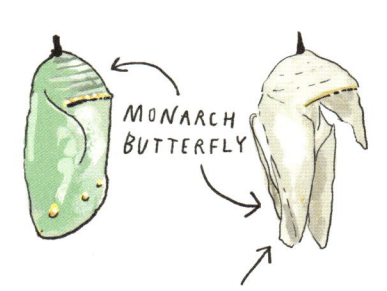

MONARCH BUTTERFLY

After the butterfly emerges, what's left is a discarded skin.

COCOON

A cocoon is like a sleeping bag for a caterpillar to hide in while it metamorphoses.

A caterpillar spins itself a protective shell out of silk and sometimes other stuff, like bits of leaf, to disguise it from predators.

When the moth is ready to emerge it has to know how to get out! Some cocoons are so sturdy that the moth has to secrete a special liquid to soften it enough to make an exit hole.

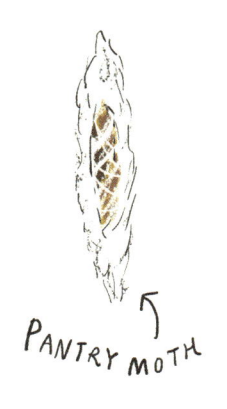

PANTRY MOTH

CATERPILLARS

Caterpillars are the larvae of moths and butterflies. It's often easier to find the larvae than the adults because they tend to stay in one place, more or less. Isn't it amazing that these are the same animal?

I can't believe I used to think that was fashionable.

Calcarifera ordinata — WATTLE CUP MOTH

Caterpillars can make silk and some of them use it like a bungee rope to get away quickly from predators. They drop off a leaf and dangle upside down in midair, hoping that by the time they've climbed back up their thread the danger has passed.

While some caterpillars have extravagantly bright skin that makes them look poisonous, others are masters of hide and seek.

CLASSIC CATERPILLAR CAMOUFLAGE

TWIG IMPERSONATION

LEAF-VEIN MIMICRY

IN SOMEONE'S EYEBROWS (just kidding)

Caterpillars are fussy eaters, so if you find one crawling up your sleeve, see if you can put it back in the right spot.

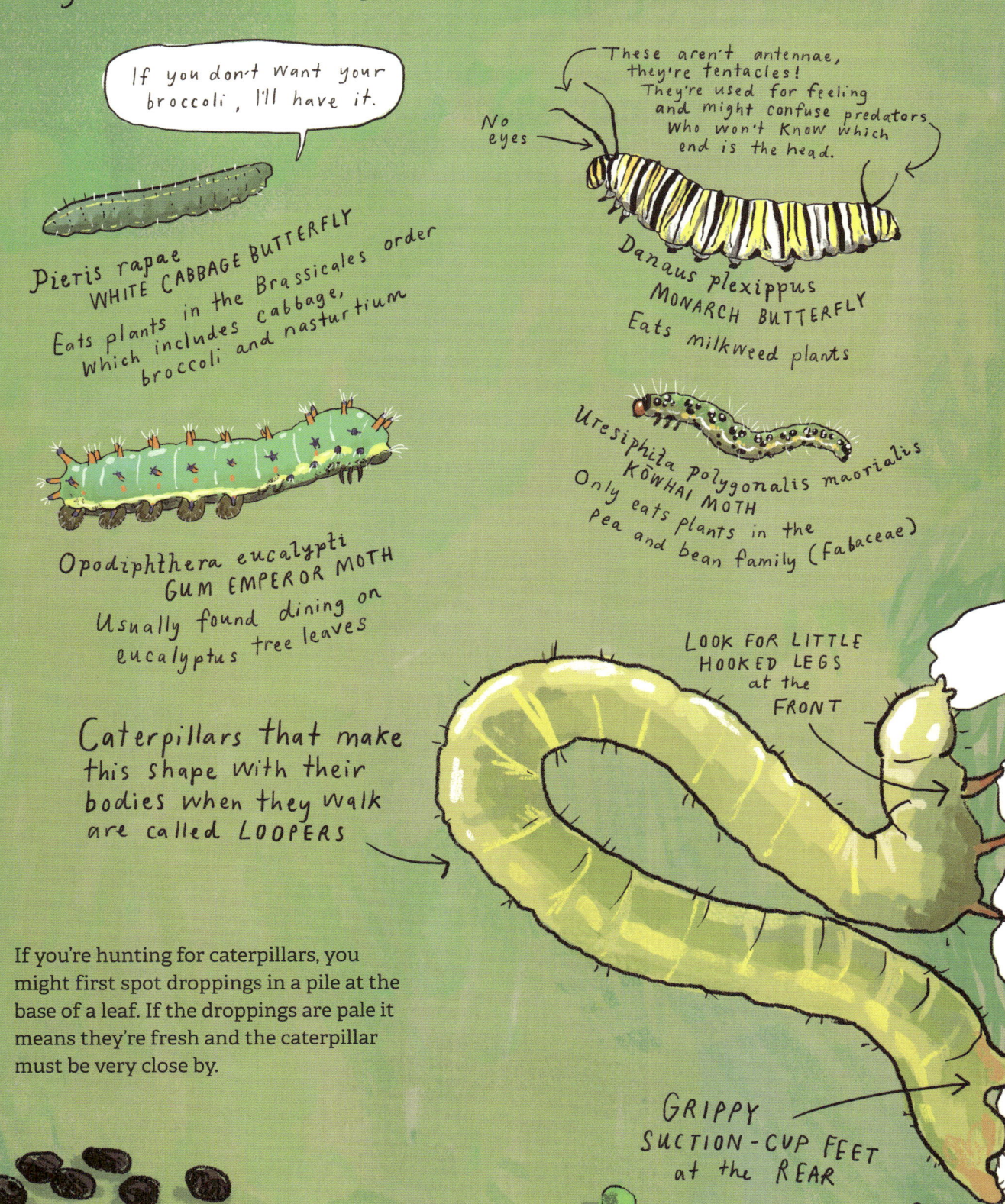

"If you don't want your broccoli, I'll have it."

Pieris rapae
WHITE CABBAGE BUTTERFLY
Eats plants in the Brassicales order which includes cabbage, broccoli and nasturtium

These aren't antennae, they're tentacles! They're used for feeling and might confuse predators who won't know which end is the head.

No eyes

Danaus plexippus
MONARCH BUTTERFLY
Eats milkweed plants

Opodiphthera eucalypti
GUM EMPEROR MOTH
Usually found dining on eucalyptus tree leaves

Uresiphita polygonalis maorialis
KŌWHAI MOTH
Only eats plants in the pea and bean family (Fabaceae)

Caterpillars that make this shape with their bodies when they walk are called LOOPERS

LOOK FOR LITTLE HOOKED LEGS at the FRONT

GRIPPY SUCTION-CUP FEET at the REAR

If you're hunting for caterpillars, you might first spot droppings in a pile at the base of a leaf. If the droppings are pale it means they're fresh and the caterpillar must be very close by.

SEEDS

KŌWHAI TREE

RED HORSE EYE SEA BEAN

A seed is hardly ever simply a little brown bead, like this broccoli seed. →

The shape, hue and size of seeds is as varied as the plants that they grow into! As big as a coconut, as tiny as the poppy seed on your bread roll. Yellow, red, spiky, flat, papery—there are seeds of every kind.

In general, a plant wants its seeds to grow as far away from it as possible. This helps the species survive because it means, for example, that every tree of a kind won't be blown down in the same storm. So plants have evolved extraordinary tricks for spreading their seeds.

Buoyant seeds can travel huge distances by floating down rivers or across oceans.

Mangrove

COCONUT (very much not to scale)

Seeds as fine as dust or with sails are carried a long way by the wind.

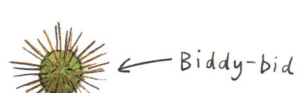

← Dandelion

↑ Foxglove

← Biddy-bid

Bristly, clingy seeds stick like Velcro. If a furry animal (or you, in long socks) brushes against them they latch on and are taken to another location.

Hairy bittercress

PEW! PEW!

Spring-loaded seeds go **BOING** and rocket off like tiny cannonballs as soon as something knocks their pod.

One of the main ways plants spread their seeds is by making delicious fruit for animals to eat. The seeds can survive being digested and then when they get pooped out, the surrounding droppings provide moisture and nutrients to help them grow.

If you accidentally swallow a seed from a piece of fruit, don't worry, it can't grow inside of you. Your bowels will move it along before it has a chance and there's not enough light in there anyway.

Poppy seed heads work like little salt and pepper shakers.

Do you like eating seeds in tomato sauce?

Peas and corn and beans are all seeds but they won't grow after being frozen, preserved or cooked.

↑ Minute specks of pollen

A grassy patch can be made of many different types of grasses that look very alike until they flower and go to seed. Each species has a unique and lovely structure. Grass flowers are called spikelets and they don't have petals. Look VERY closely to spot them!

Honesty seeds come perfectly pressed in a tissue-thin envelope

Cape gooseberry seeds in their little lace bag

A fresh oak seed comes with a hat.

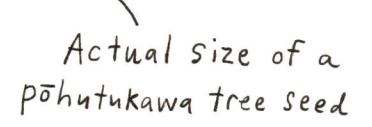

← Actual size of a pōhutukawa tree seed

That seed 100 years later

89

NOTABLE LEAVES

These are leaflets

This is a leaf

A clover leaf is TRIFOLATE because it has three parts. Unless it's a four-leafed clover, which is QUATREFOILED.

When all the flesh rots away and only lacy veins are left, you get a SKELETON LEAF

These bits protrude like earlobes.

LOBATE LEAF

False leaf (it's a katydid)

FEATHERY LEAF

Your nose can help you to identify plants.

Crush a leaf and sniff it. They don't all smell the same.

You can try doing this with fresh cooking herbs to test yourself.

Blistery looking leaf from a Peach tree that's been infected by a fungus.

Needle (a very pointy leaf)

Delicious leaf

SERRATED LEAF

Jagged edges like a saw blade.

You don't have to go to the zoo to see interesting animals. Is there a little spider in the corner of your hallway, or something helping itself to scraps in your kitchen? Maybe something came zooming in through the window and can't find its way back out again. Observology can be a delightfully lazy activity; you don't even have to go outside.

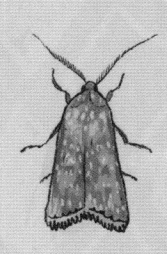

BEHIND THE CURTAINS

COCKROACHES

When you think of a cockroach you probably picture the brown critter that scuttles away when you open the cupboard under the stairs for the first time in forever. They don't like light, so the sudden brightness drives the cockroach away in search of a dark, narrow crevice in which to hide its conveniently flat body.

Some cockroach species have a poor reputation because they've learnt that humans are a wonderful source of food, and they like to live in our well-stocked kitchens and bins. But there are over 4000 types of cockroach in the world and only a few are considered a nuisance. A lot of them aren't even brown.

Hurry up and turn the page, it's too bright!

A few species, that is... not a few ill-mannered individuals.

Common household cockroaches
(and a lesson in being wary of common names)

Would absence make your heart grow fonder?

Periplaneta americana
AMERICAN COCKROACH
(Actually native to Africa)

No wonder my Deutsch grammar is so bad.

Blatta orientalis
ORIENTAL COCKROACH
(Possibly from Russia)

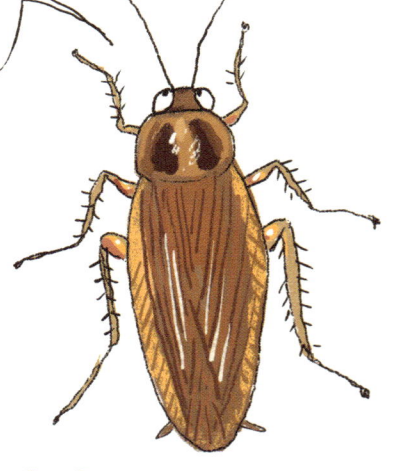

Blattella germanica
GERMAN COCKROACH
(Thought to be native to North Africa, or maybe Asia)

NOT common household cockroaches

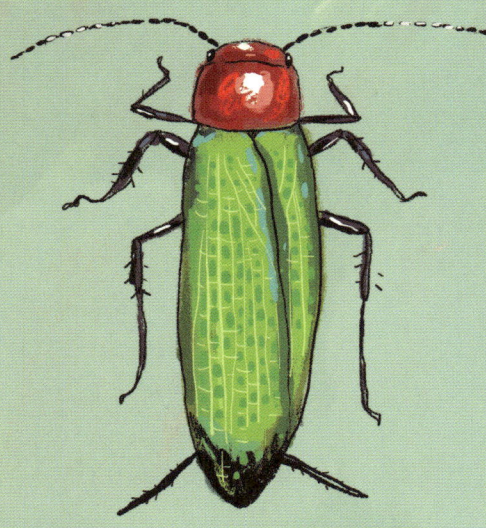

Melyroidea magnifica
BLISTER BEETLE
MIMIC COCKROACH
(South America)

Therea petiveriana
DOMINO COCKROACH
(India and Sri Lanka)

"Would you think I was yucky if I lived in your cupboard?"

Juvenile form of
Ellipsidion australe
ELLIPSIDION COCKROACH
(Australia)

Panchlora nivea
GREEN BANANA COCKROACH
(Cuba)

Drymaplaneta semivitta, the Gisborne cockroach (native to Australia)

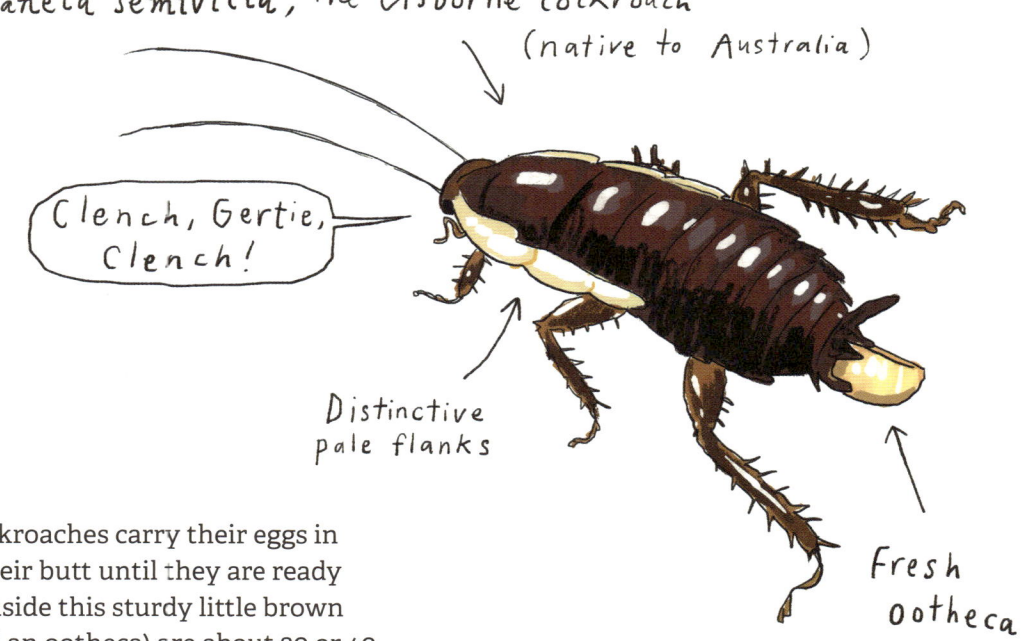

"Clench, Gertie, Clench!"

Distinctive pale flanks

Fresh ootheca

Female cockroaches carry their eggs in a case in their butt until they are ready to hatch. Inside this sturdy little brown case (called an ootheca) are about 30 or 40 individual eggs. Praying mantises are not-too-distantly related to cockroaches and they lay oothecae too.

The Gisborne cockroach tends to be a loner. American cockroaches, by contrast, are gregarious insects, meaning that they live in social groups. Scientists watching the way they behave have found reasons to believe that each cockroach has its own personality!

8mm

American cockroach ootheca

"LET'S PARTY!"

"Thanks but I'd rather eat my book."

As a young cockroach grows it sheds its skin. Underneath this discarded outer layer it is squishy and milky white. While it waits for this fresh layer to harden, it is VERY vulnerable and easy for something to sink its teeth into. Even another cockroach might not be able to resist having a nibble.

Quite angelic

A beautiful green fly
with long legs

(actual size)

FLIES

Calliphora vomitoria
BLUE BOTTLE FLY
You don't have to want it near your sandwiches, but isn't it a pretty blue?

Flies come in an almost infinite range of shapes and sizes. Some of the prettiest ones are the least popular because they can spread diseases.

This is a very good restaurant, they never skimp on the maggots.

How wonderful!

It's entirely reasonable not to want a fly laying its eggs on your lunch, but a special kind of cheese is infested with fly eggs on purpose. The maggots that hatch are what make the cheese so delicious. Everyone has their own preferences, of course.

DRONE FLIES

Many flies are important pollinators, doing the work that bees often get credit for. This drone fly even looks a lot like a bee! Its larvae are called rat-tailed maggots. The maggots live in pools of stagnant water full of rotting leaves. What looks like a tail is actually a snorkel. The tip is always out of the water so the maggot can breathe. How clever.

I'm sort of an honorary bee.

ADULT DRONE FLY

HUFF PUFF

YOUNG DRONE FLY

Some particularly magnificent flies are the minuscule midges of the genus *Forcipomyia*, responsible for pollinating the flowers of the cacao tree, the source of chocolate! The cacao flowers are small and awkwardly shaped, so it's not a job just any insect can do. Remember to thank a fly the next time you eat a yummy chocolate muffin.

I should be your number one animal.

A CACAO FLOWER

BACKSTROKE!

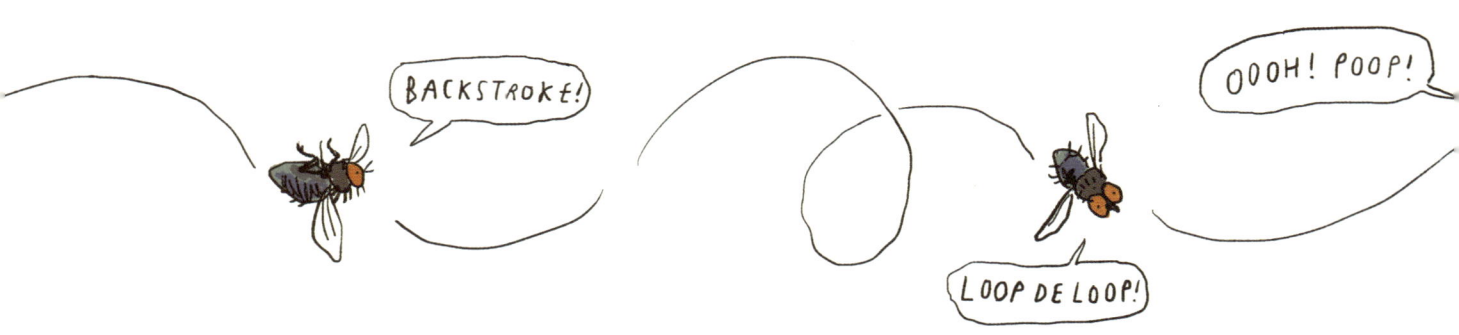

LOOP DE LOOP!

OOOH! POOP!

You think it's cold but it's actually ennui.

Insects like bees and butterflies have two pairs of wings, but flies have only one pair. That's why the order they belong to is called Diptera, meaning "two-winged". Where their second set of wings would have been, they evolved parts called halteres. These specialized flight instruments, which look like maracas, help a fly keep its balance in the air. That's why flies are so good at aerobatics and VERY hard to catch in mid-air.

Common household flies prefer warm temperatures. When the weather's cold you might see very sluggish flies sitting in the same spot on the windowsill for several days.

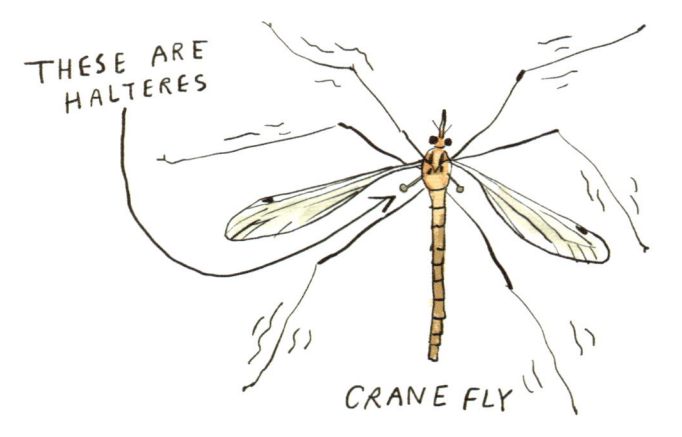

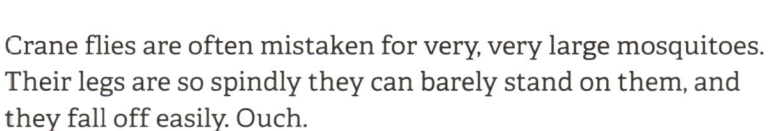

THESE ARE HALTERES

CRANE FLY

First Class BOARDING PASS BATWAYS FLIGHT 459

Crane flies are often mistaken for very, very large mosquitoes. Their legs are so spindly they can barely stand on them, and they fall off easily. Ouch.

Not all flies have wings, which sounds RIDICULOUS, but it's true. The bat fly is a fly with no wings, but technically it can still fly because it lives in the fur of bats.

Mystacinobia zelandica
WINGLESS BATFLY

The FRUIT FLY

The common fruit fly is sometimes mistaken for a pest. But it only hangs around fruit that's already rotting and it's totally harmless. It lives in every country on earth!

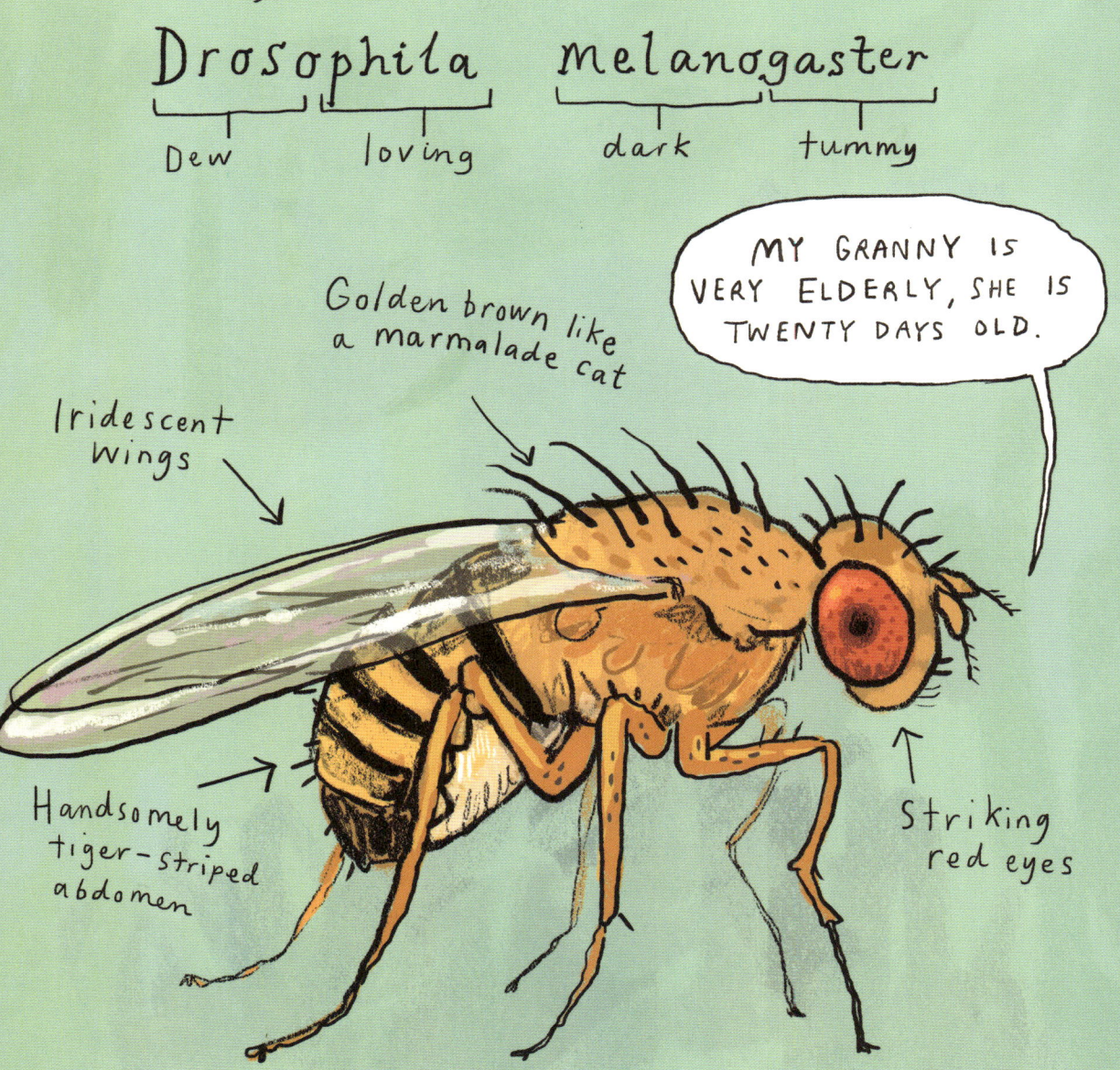

Drosophila melanogaster
Dew | loving | dark | tummy

Iridescent wings

Golden brown like a marmalade cat

"MY GRANNY IS VERY ELDERLY, SHE IS TWENTY DAYS OLD."

Handsomely tiger-striped abdomen

Striking red eyes

Fruit flies are VERY popular with scientists because they're easy to look after and they grow and breed so quickly. They're great for studying patterns in genetics, because a new generation is produced every ten days or so!

"YOO-HOO!" ← Actual size

AURAL OBSERVOLOGY

If you listen carefully, you'll soon realize that you recognize different insects just from the sound they make. Not all buzzes are alike, and you have very clever ears.

nnnnNN

HOmm

Dragonfly wings slap the air and make a sound like winding up a toy car. By the way, dragonflies are not a type of fly! You can tell because they have four wings; flies have two.

SK SK SK

ZIZZIZZIZzz

The buzz of a housefly changes slightly every time it changes direction.

ZIZZIZZZ ZIZZZZZ ZZZZZ

mmzzzz

NNNNNNNNNNNNNNNNNNNN Mosquitoes make a high-pitched whine. It's fairly annoying.

MBBB Bombus — the scientific name for bumblebees — comes from an Ancient Greek word "bombos", meaning a humming or buzzing sound. It is the perfect word because when you say it your whole mouth feels like a bumblebee.

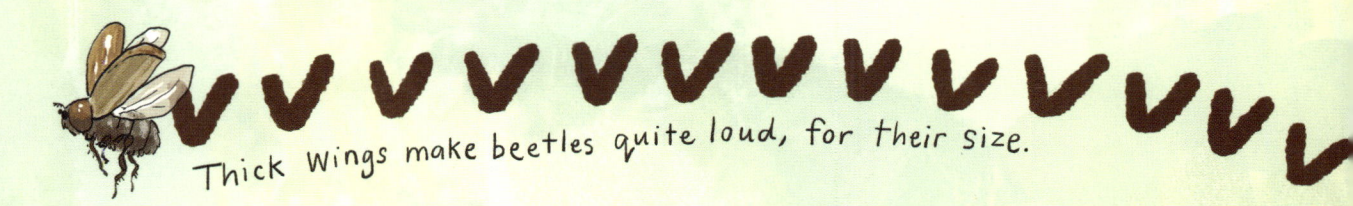

SK SK SK SK SK SK SK SK SK SK SK SK SK SK SK SK SK SK

vvvvvvvvvvvvvvvvvv Thick wings make beetles quite loud, for their size.

Honey bees have a much higher-pitched buzz than bumblebees. zzmmmmmmmmzzzzzm

SPIDERS

Unlike flying creatures, many spiders stay in much the same place for ages, so you can get to know an individual spider's routines and preferences. If there's one living nearby you can visit it every day and give it a name.

Scientifically, we know of more than 50,000 species of spider. Only about 25 of these have a bite considered dangerous to humans. It's important to know if any of these ones live near you, but spiders don't deserve their reputation for being scary.

People tend to focus on the spiders that are so big and venomous they can eat mice and birds, but most spiders are small and cute and eat other tiny invertebrates. Spiders like this can't even pierce human skin.

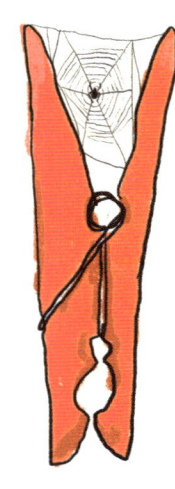

Venomous means that a creature can inject its prey with venom when it bites or stings.

Poisonous is the word for something that is toxic if it is eaten (or touched, like some particularly spectacular frogs).

You might see jumping spiders like these roaming around your walls. They don't build webs, they hunt instead. They're fun to watch.

Help.

A jumping spider sitting on a kernel of corn (actual size)

I CALL DIBS!

No way, I saw it first.

Australia is famous for its venomous spiders, but maybe it should be famous for its dancing peacock spiders instead.

- A type of jumping spider
- Just one of many species of peacock spider
- Harmless to people
- The male spider does an elaborate dance to woo its mate
- Glorious!

Maratus volans

ACTUAL SIZE

HOW TO WIN THE LOVE OF A JUMPING SPIDER*

WAGGLE WAGGLE

SHUFFLE SHUFFLE

FLICK! FLICK!

*Results not guaranteed

105

When a spider lowers itself to the ground, look how it uses its back leg to carefully control its descent.

A CONSTELLATION OF BABY SPIDERS

Spider silk comes out of spinnerets at the tip of the spider's abdomen. All spiders can make silk, but they don't all use it to make webs. Spiders make different types of silk for different purposes.

SPINNERETS
(spider butt, top view)

Silk for safely swaddling eggs

Silk for wrapping food

Silk safety rope

Watch a spider climbing a wall and you'll see its bum tap the wall every few steps. It's putting in an anchor made of silk so that if it slips it won't fall far, just like rock climbers do with their rope gear.

A spider's web is made of really strong silk, but the spider makes special extra-sticky stuff to weave into the part designed to catch prey.

Spiders eat their own webs if they need to. Their silk is made of proteins that their bodies can recycle into a fresh batch of silk and a lovely new web.

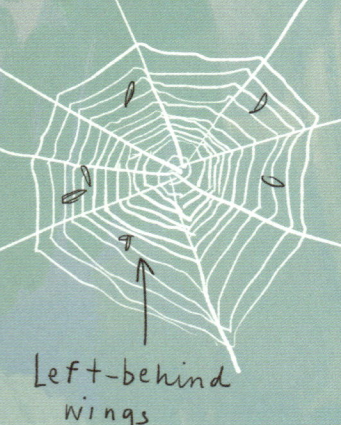

Left-behind wings

LOOK! Infinite silk!

ALMOST INVISIBLE SILK THREAD

If you want to pick up a very small spider without squishing it, try pinching the air just behind its back end to grab hold of its silk thread instead.

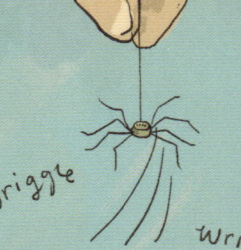

wriggle
wriggle

106

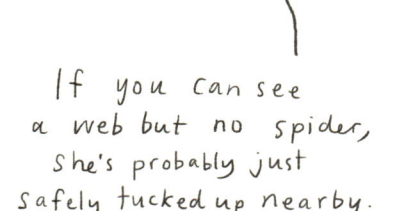

If you can see a web but no spider, she's probably just safely tucked up nearby.

There's a myth saying that daddy-long-legs spiders are extremely venomous but too weak to pierce human skin. It's not true! Daddy-long-legs spiders can be venomous to a small number of other creatures, but they won't hurt you; in fact they're built so delicately, it's more likely the other way around. They are hard to hold on to, like trying to catch a single hair in a strong breeze with mittens on.

Spiders don't have antennae but they do have pedipalps on their faces. These are very sensitive and can pick up tastes and smells, and male spiders use theirs to give sperm to female spiders. Look closely and you'll see them twitch and waggle.

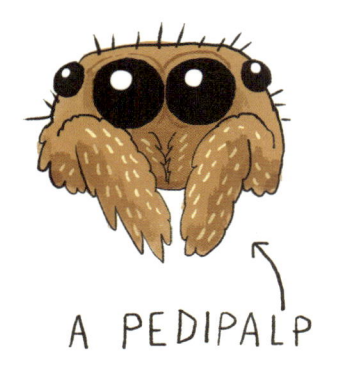

We're used to seeing animals with two eyes that are always in approximately the same place on their head. Most spiders have eight eyes, but some have fewer. The arrangement of eyes varies depending on the species.

A PEDIPALP

SOME DIFFERENT SPIDER EYE FORMATIONS

Entomophagy is the practice of humans eating insects (on purpose, that is), and most spiders do it too. There is, however, at least one vegetarian spider in the world. It lives in Mexico and Costa Rica and eats little protein-rich knobbly bits off acacia trees. It is named *Bagheera kiplingi*, after the black panther from *The Jungle Book* by Rudyard Kipling. Panthers are not vegetarian.

Bagheera kiplingi

DIFFERENT WEBS FOR DIFFERENT SPIDERS

Spiders are wonderful engineers and build webs in lots of different forms. Here are just a few of them. It's usually only female spiders that build webs. Occasionally you'll see a male spider on a web, inching cautiously towards a female he'd like to mate with. He has to plan his approach carefully because in many cases male spiders are much smaller than the females. If he annoys her, she might eat him.

Very orderly

A snug home for the whole family

Young nursery web spiders

Messy but effective

Flat on the ground

A particularly good time to look at spider webs is on a dewy morning. Each silk thread hangs heavy with tiny, sparkling beads of water. It's very pretty.

HOW TO RELOCATE A SPIDER

This method works nicely for most creatures small enough to fit in a cup.

You need: a clear plastic container or cup with a nice wide mouth, and a piece of paper.

First, locate your spider. When it's sitting against a flat surface (like the floor, wall, or window) carefully place the container over it.

Lift this very slightly

Sliiiide

Gently slide the piece of paper underneath the container, taking care not to jostle the spider too roughly.

Hold the paper firmly over the mouth of the container while you carry the spider outside.

Let it go! Good job, have a treat.

HOW TO SAVE A MOTH FROM DROWNING WITHOUT ACCIDENTALLY MAKING THE SITUATION WORSE

If there's running water, make things easier by turning it off.

Try to scoop your hand underneath the moth; don't pinch it with your fingers (that will definitely make the situation worse).

Gently transfer the moth onto a piece of tissue, which will help dry its wings.

Leave the moth on the tissue and take it outside. Hopefully the moth will fly away, but don't be too disheartened if it doesn't. You tried your best.

MOTHS

The world is home to many beautiful, ornate and fancy moths. It's not true that all butterflies are bright and all moths are dull. People who like to dress up as butterfly princesses should consider being a moth princess next time.

Moths (and butterflies) are in the order Lepidoptera. If you pick up a moth you might notice that it leaves dust on your fingers. The dust is actually tiny little scales that cover moths' wings, so delicate they fall off easily when they're brushed or knocked. These scales give moths their patterns and it's possible they're used as a sense organ too. The name Lepidoptera comes from Greek words meaning *scale wing*.

Anyway, even if a lot of moths ARE brown, brown can be warm and lovely. The brown moths on the opposite page all boast subtle, ornate patterns and delicate shapes. They are magnificent in a quiet way.

Nocturnal moths evolved with only the light of the moon to guide them, so brightly lit streets and houses confuse them. That's why they end up coming inside at night, or tap-tap-tapping at your windows, asking to be let in (don't let them in, they don't know what's good for them!).

Clever animals that like to eat moths (such as owls, bats and spiders) have learnt to hang around well-lit places at night.

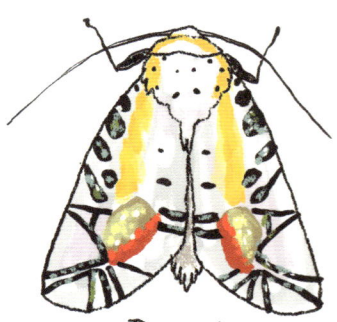

Utetheisa ornatrix
RATTLEBOX MOTH

Baorisa hieroglyphica
PICASSO MOTH

Dull patch where the scales have worn off

BIRTHDAY PRESENT IDEAS FOR YOUR FRIEND WHO IS AN OWL
• Headlamp

Nice zig-zags
Feathery fringe like on a rug
Looks like wood
Shaped like an arrowhead. Where is it pointing you?
Narrow and Shimmery
Also looks like wood but in a different way
Tiny
This one's got a tuft

Most moths you see in your house got there by accident. But some are there on purpose.

CARPET MOTH

In the wild the larvae of these moths eat birds' nests and old animal skins, but they've found that houses are snug and that carpet made of wool is a very satisfactory meal.

PANTRY MOTH

Also called the Indian meal moth, the larvae eat dried grains and there's no place they'd rather live than in a well-stocked pantry.

No need to fret, madame, I don't like omelettes.

MOTH EGGS

If a female moth is in mortal peril she will drop all the eggs she's carrying so that there's a chance her offspring will survive even if she doesn't.

CLOTHES MOTH

Like the carpet moth's, these larvae enjoy a healthy diet of natural fabric, which means that your nice winter cardigan looks like dinner for the whole family.

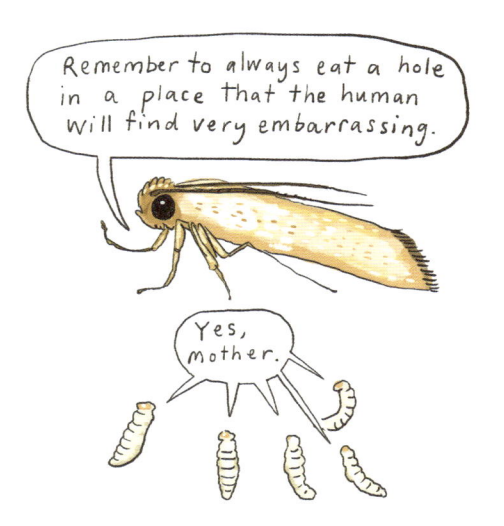

Remember to always eat a hole in a place that the human will find very embarrassing.

Yes, mother.

Some moths, like the clothes moth, don't have a mouth when they're adults. What a fate!

The taste of long underwear is but a sweet memory...

NOT ALL MOTHS are nocturnal; plenty of moths do their moth things during daylight hours.

A little diurnal moth eating and pollinating flowers.
There are flowers that bloom at night and there are moths that visit them too.

MOTHS vs. BUTTERFLIES

There are exceptions to these rules, so no one feature on its own will identify your mystery Lepidoptera, but if it has more in common with the moth column, it's probably a moth. And vice versa.

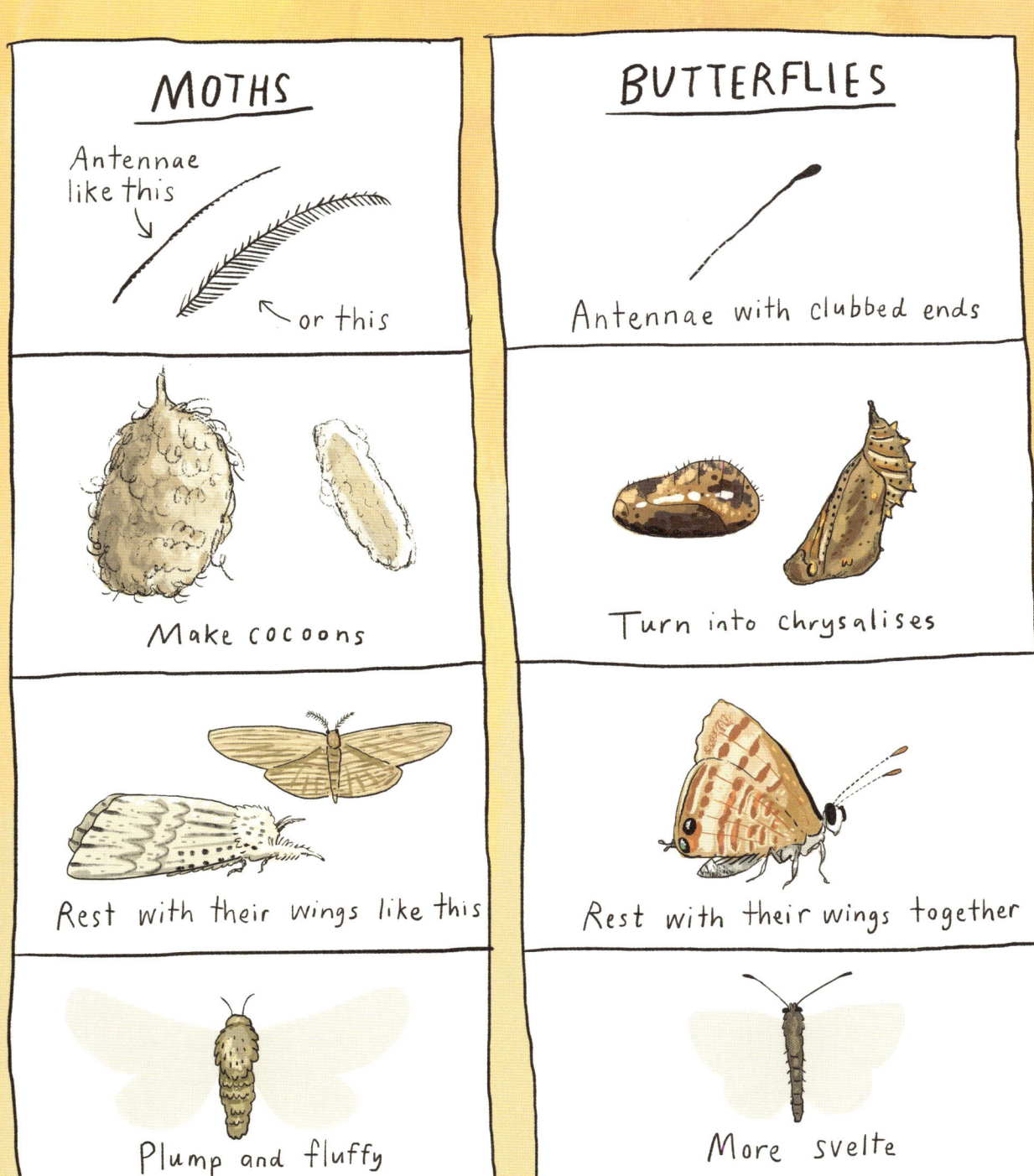

MOTHS	BUTTERFLIES
Antennae like this → ← or this	Antennae with clubbed ends
Make cocoons	Turn into chrysalises
Rest with their wings like this	Rest with their wings together
Plump and fluffy	More svelte

AN OBSERVOLOGIST'S FINAL EXAM

① What are you?

    A. Enormous   B. Curious

    C. A nice creature   D. Thoughtful

② What are you looking for?

    A. Small things   B. Very small things

    C. Extremely small things   D. Almost absurdly small things

③ Why?

    A. Because I want to   B. Because they're cool

    C. Because the more you learn the more interesting everything is   D. No reason, it's just an inherently neat activity

④ Where will you find things to observe?

    A. Under your nose   B. Everywhere

    C. Over there   D. I'm pointing to something now

⑤ What is the world?

    A. Magnificent   B. Spectacular

    C. Weird   D. Remarkable in every way

100%

WELL DONE!

Did you notice the 13 little red spider mites running through this book? You've probably been an observologist all along.

This is to certify that

has completed the required course of study to be awarded the qualification of

OBSERVOLOGIST

IN THE YEAR

and is hereby granted the authority to perform observology here, there and everywhere.

Department of Observology

INDEX

aerobatics, 100
African giant millipedes, 39
age, 101
algae, 58
American cockroaches
  (*Periplaneta americana*), 94, 96
Antarctica, 58
antennae, 19, 23, 37, 51, 53, 77, 115
ants, 7, 9–11, 50–53, 63
aphids, 7, 10
aquatic worms, 41
Asian paper wasps (*Polistes chinensis*), 79
Australia, 28, 50, 67, 95–96, 105

backswimmer, 40
bacteria, 58
bat flies, 100
bats, 112
bees, 11, 22, 43, 50, 62, 71–77, 99, 103
beetles, 6, 8, 15, 20, 34, 41, 57, 69, 85
big blue earthworm
  (*Terriswalkeris terraereginae*), 67
bird dropping spider, 46
bird poop, 49, 53–55
birds, 15, 18, 43, 48, 54–55, 61, 71, 104
biting creatures, 38, 104
Bittium (sea snail), 15
black household ant, 50
blackbirds, 66
blister beetle mimic cockroaches, 95
blowflies, 85, 99
body parts, 19–23, 28, 37, 51, 65, 77, 84, 101, 107
Boops boops (fish), 15
breathing, 22, 41, 65, 69
bristles, 4, 17, 65
bull ants, 50
bullet ants, 50
bumblebees (*Bombus*), 73–75, 103.
  see also bees
butterflies, 22, 43, 46, 57, 62–63, 85–87, 112, 115
buzzing, 77, 102

cabbage white butterflies
  (*Pieris rapae*), 85, 87
cacao flowers, 99
caddisfly larvae, 47
camouflage, 46–47, 86, 90.
  see also hiding places
carnivores, 38
carpenter bees, 76
carpet moths, 114
caterpillars, 6, 10, 28, 62, 69, 78–79, 85–86
centipedes, 21, 38
cephalothorax, 21
cerebral ganglion, 28
chafer beetles, 20
cheese, 35, 99
chocolate, 99
chrysalises, 84–85, 115
cicadas, 80, 84
cleaning, 73
clitellum, 65
cloaca, 55
clothes moths, 114
clover, 90
cockroaches, 62–63, 94–97
cocoons, 8, 66, 84–85, 115

collections, 56
colonies, 50, 78
colossal squid, 18, 26
common earthworms
  (*Lumbricus terrestris*), 66
common garden snails (*Cornu aspersum*), 31
common wasps (*Vespula vulgaris*), 77–78
communication, 53
compost bins, 35, 66
compound eyes, 22, 37, 51
copepods, 40
courtship, 105
crabs, 18, 36, 47
crane flies, 100
crayfish, 36
crickets, 43, 63
crinoline stinkhorn (*Phallus indusiatus*), 32
crepuscular creatures, 43
crustaceans, 36
cuckoo wasps (*Chrysura refulgens*), 79

daddy-long-legs, 14, 107
damp habitats, 6, 24–25, 27, 29, 32, 36, 40
damsel flies, 20, 41
dances, 105
dandelions, 17, 88
decision making, 81
deserts, 58
diet, 11, 27, 32, 34, 37–39, 50, 53, 55, 61, 66, 73–74, 78, 87, 94, 106, 114
digger bees, 76
diseases, 99
dispersal, 88
diurnal creatures, 43, 114
diving beetles, 41
domino cockroaches, 95
dragonflies, 22, 57, 102
drawing, 17
drone flies, 99
drones, 73
droppings, 9, 62, 66, 87, 88. *see also* bird poop
drowning, saving moths from, 111

earthworms, 62–68. *see also* worms
eating. *see* diet
egg cases, 96
eggs, 41, 50, 52, 56, 63, 66, 79, 84, 96, 106, 114
ellipisidion cockroaches, 95
engineering, 108
entomophagy (eating insects), 107
epiphragm, 30
evolutionary family tree, 12–13
exoskeleton, 19
expeditions, 4, 6
eyes, 22, 37, 42, 51, 73, 107

fairy's toothbrush, 81
feathers, 56
feelers. *see* antennae
feelings, 64
fig wasps (*Ceratosolen capensis*), 79
fish, 15, 18
flies (Diptera), 11, 14, 41, 43, 62–63, 71, 98–101
fly agaric mushrooms
  (*Amanita muscaria*), 34
fly spray, 11
fly traps, 34
flying, 100. *see also* wings
food. *see* diet
fortune telling, 81
foxgloves, 88
frass, 62. *see also* droppings

freshwater snails, 40
frogs, 46, 69, 104
fruit flies
  (*Drosophila melanogaster*), 100–101
fruits, 78, 88
fungal infections, 91
fungi, 4, 24, 32–35, 42, 58

gaster, 51
gastropods, 26–28
geese, 13
Gelae baen (beetle), 15
Gelae fish (beetle), 15
genetics, 101
German cockroaches
  (*Blatella germanica*), 94
German wasps, 78
giraffe weevils, 6
Gisborne cockroaches
  (*Drymaplaneta semivitta*), 96
glow-in-the-dark mushroom
  (*Armillaria novae-zelandiae*), 32
golden spider wasps
  (*Cryptocheilus australis*), 79
grains, 114
grasshoppers, 69
Greek, 15, 103, 112
green banana cockroaches, 95
gregarious insects, 96
grey garden slugs
  (*Deroceras reticulatum*), 26
growing up, 84–87, 97, 101
grubs, 34, 85
guano, 43, 55. *see also* bird poop
gull pellet, 54
gum emperor moths
  (*Opodiphthera eucalypti*), 87

habitats, 6, 24–25, 27, 29, 32, 36, 40, 48, 58, 70–71, 92–93
haemolymph, 19
hagfishes, 13
halteres, 100
head lice, 20
hearing, 22
help, how to, 64, 68, 75
hermaphrodites, 28, 65
hiding places, 29, 36, 94.
  see also camouflage
hives, 73, 78
homes, bee, 76
honey, 78
honey bees (*Apis mellifera*), 73, 77, 103.
  see also bees
hoopoe bird (*Upupa epops*), 15
houseflies, 102. *see also* flies
humans (*Homo sapiens*), 13, 19
humidity, 73

Indian meal moths, 114
indoor habitats, 6, 92–93
insect sounds, 77, 102
insects, 17–20, 22–24, 48. *see also* bees; beetles; butterflies; flies; moths; wasps
insects, as food, 107
instruments, observology, 16
invertebrates, 18, 22
Ittibittium (sea snail), 15

jellyfish, 47
jumping spiders, 104–105

katydids, 90
Kipling, Rudyard, 107
kōwhai moths
(*Uresiphita polygonalis maorialis*), 87

ladybirds, 10
larvae, 41, 50, 52, 79, 84–86, 114
Latin, 15, 63
leaf-cutter bees, 76
leaves, 9–10, 56, 60, 90–91
leeches, 40
legs, 14, 17, 21, 37–39, 51, 73–74, 100
lemon tree borer parasites
(*Xanthocryptus novozealandicus*), 79
leopard slugs (*Limax maximus*), 6, 27
lichens, 17, 48, 56, 58–59
light, 16, 22, 43, 45, 112
little brown mushrooms (LBMs), 34
lizards, 18
loopers, 87

maggots, 85, 99
mandibles, 51
mantle, 28
mating, 42, 61, 73, 107–108
matutinal creatures, 43
metamorphosis, 85
mice, 104
midges, 99
millipedes, 21, 38–39, 71
monarch butterflies
(*Danaus plexippus*), 79, 85, 87
mosquitoes, 41, 100, 103
moss, 17
moths, 4, 8, 42–43, 63, 71, 84–87, 111–115
mould, 35
mouthparts, 50–51, 73, 114
movement, 28, 37–41, 64, 87, 100, 102, 106
Mt Kaputar pink slug, 28
mushrooms, 32–34

names, scientific, 14–15
nectar, 73
nests, 61, 78–79, 114
nocturnal creatures, 24, 29, 42–43, 112
nursery web spiders, 108
nymphs, 80, 84

observology principles, 8
octopuses, 12, 15, 26
ommatidia, 22
ootheca (egg case), 96
opalescence, 66
orange ichneumonid wasps
(*Netelia ephippiata*), 79
orchid mantises, 46
oriental cockroaches (*Blatta orientalis*), 94
ovipositors, 63
owls, 54, 112

pantry moths, 85, 114
paper wasps, 78
parasitoid wasps, 79
pavement habitats, 6, 48–50, 58
peacock spiders (*Maratus volans*), 105
pedicel, 21
pedipalps, 21, 107
pellets (vomited), 54
periwinkle flowers, 81
personality, 96
pest control, 78
pesticides, 11

petiole, 51
phenology, 16, 60–61
pheromones, 53
Philippine fried egg worm
(*Archipherelima middletoni*), 21
photosensitive cells, 65
Picasso moth (*Baorisa hieroglyphica*), 112
pill millipedes, 39
plankton, 40
plant growth, 60
plantain pea shooter, 81
plants, 4, 17, 32
plasterer bees, 76
playing dead, 57
pneumostome, 28
poisonous things, 32, 86, 104
pollinators, 71–79, 99, 114
ponds, 40
poop. *see* droppings
praying mantises, 57, 63, 84, 96
predators, 44, 78, 85–87, 106
pterostigma (wing part), 57
puddles, 40
pupae, 52, 84–85
pure green sweat bee, 74

queen ants, 50
queen bees, 73
queen wasps, 78

rain, 64, 83
rat-tailed maggots, 99
rattlebox moths (*Utetheisa ornatrix*), 112
recycling, 32
red spider mites, 1, 6, 14, 17, 28, 34, 46, 55, 65, 81, 90, 112, 116
relocating spiders, 110
reproduction, 28, 59, 65–66, 101, 107–108
rescuing moths, 111
robber fly, 20
rose thorn rhino horn, 80

safety, 8
safety ropes, 106
scales, 112
scientific names, 14–15
scientists, 4, 14–15, 32, 34, 55, 64, 96, 101
sea cucumbers, 13
sea slugs, 26
sea snails, 15, 30
seasonal patterns, 60–61
seeds, 56, 88–89
segmented bodies, 21, 36–39
senses, 22, 53, 64–65, 107, 112
shells, 30, 56
shrimps, 36
silk, 85–86, 106
sinistral shells, 30
skin, 65
skin shedding, 80, 84–85, 97
slater spider (*Dysdera crocata*), 37
slaters. *see* wood lice
slime, 9, 24, 28, 30
slugs (mollusks), 4, 6, 10, 21, 26–30, 34, 42, 62–63, 69, 83
smells, 53, 91, 107
snails (mollusks), 10, 12, 21, 26, 28–31, 34, 42, 62–63, 83
sneaking up (on bugs), 69
snorkels, 99
solitary bees, 74
song thrush, Eurasian (*Turdus philomelos*), 15

sounds, 77, 102
sparrows, 61
species, 12–13, 15, 32, 66, 74, 76, 78, 94, 104
spider skins, 56
spiders (arachnids), 8, 14, 17, 21, 37, 42, 44, 46, 62–63, 71, 78–79, 83, 104–110, 112
spinnerets, 106
spiracles, 22
spiral directions, 30
spores, 33, 59
stalking, 69
stick insects, 20
stingers, 50–51, 57, 63
stinging, 73, 104
stingless bees, 74
stink bugs, 10
sugar syrup, 75
surface tension, 83
sycamore seed propeller, 80

tardigrades, 7, 59
taste receptors, 22, 107
taxonomy, 12
temperature, 100
tentacles, 4, 28, 87
territory, 61
thanatosis (playing dead), 57
The Jungle Book, 107
tiger worms (*Eisenia fetida*), 66
toadstools, 32
tortoise beetles, 6
touch, 65
trees, 60
Tyrannosaurus rex (dinosaur), 15

vegetarian spider (*Bagheera kiplingi*), 107
vegetarians, 39, 107
venom, 50, 104–105, 107
vermicast, 66
vertebrates, 18
vespertine creatures, 43
vibrations, 22
violet coral (*Clavaria zollingeri*), 32
vulture bees, 74

wasps, 11, 50, 56–57, 77–79
water, 24, 26, 73
water, walking on, 83
water bears. *see* tardigrades
water boatman, 40
wattle cup moth (*Calcarifera ordinata*), 86
wavelengths, 22
weather, 60–61, 100
webs, 44, 106–109
weedy habitats, 6, 70–71
weevils, 6
welcome mat, 11
wet days, 83
white butterflies.
see cabbage white butterflies
white mushrooms (*Agaricus bisporus*), 33
wings, 19, 56–57, 77, 100–101, 112–113, 115
wood lice, 4, 11, 36–37, 71
wool, 114
wool carder bees, 76
worker ants, 50–51
worm charming, 66
worm handling, 68
worms (annelids), 4, 11, 21, 28, 41, 64–68, 71
Wunderpus photogenicus (octopus), 15

yeast, 35

Only an observologist would be reading THIS page.

First American edition published 2024

This edition first published in 2023 by Gecko Press
An imprint of Lerner Publishing Group, Inc.
241 First Avenue North, Minneapolis, MN 55401 USA

Reprinted 2024

© Gecko Press Ltd 2023
Text & illustrations © Giselle Clarkson 2023

All rights reserved. No part of this publication may be reproduced or transmitted or utilized in any form, or by any means, electronic, mechanical, photocopying or otherwise, without the prior written permission of the publisher.

The author asserts their moral right to be identified as the author of the work.

Gecko Press aims to publish with a low environmental impact. Our books are printed using vegetable inks on FSC-certified paper from sustainably managed forests. We produce books of high quality with sewn bindings and beautiful paper—made to be read over and over.

The author and publisher acknowledge the generous support of Creative New Zealand

Design and typesetting by Vida Kelly
Printed in China by Everbest Printing Co. Ltd, an accredited ISO 14001 & FSC-certified printer

ISBN 9781776575190
Ebook available

For more curiously good books, visit geckopress.com